MY DAILY ADVENTURES WITH GOD

by

Herticine Goree

Published by:
Christian Services Network
833 Broadway, Suite #201
El Cajon, CA 92021
Toll Free: 1-866-484-6184
www.CSNbooks.com

Unless otherwise stated all Scripture is taken from the King James Version of the Bible.

Printed in the United States of America.

TABLE OF CONTENTS

v

INTRODUCTION

Life has many mysteries we do not understand or willing to recognize, until we seek God in His fullness. We know something is missing, but until we seek God's revealing power they will stay disguised. During a thirty two day daily walk with God many hidden secrets within me were tapped into. Fountains of Living Water sprung forth and I could hear God's voice clearly among the many things in my surrounding. God was carrying me through this daily adventure, so He could reveal the hidden jewels inside of me. Through this walk, God taught me how to look at the simple things of nature, and He used them to break a way the hardness of my heart, which was keeping me from His presence.

With my daily walk with God, He would show me how the simple things in nature worked together for His purpose. God showed me how the flowers and birds obeyed His will. Each day the works of the Master's hands was correcting a little piece of my hardness. I was looking at the world with soiled glasses, but each day, He was cleaning them so I could see myself through His eyes. By watching the things in nature, God was rebirthing me for a special purpose in this time of my life. Concealed talents were deep inside of me and God has chosen this season to bring them forth for His kingdom. God used the trouble-free things of life to mold me into a stronger and less fearing vessel to be used by Him. I was asking for the scales to be removed from my eyes so I could see Him, however, God showed me myself first, in order for me to see Him.

God's patience through this walk taught me to depend on Him rather than myself. His patience is my salvation. The joy I experienced in the presence of the Lord was out of this world. Walking in the sweet presence of God is something the mouth cannot tell, but the heart must feel. No amount of words can explain how it felt to walk daily with God- seeing the workings of His hands-seeing the things only God can reveal that the natural eye cannot conceive. God took me by the hand and guided me to a peace I did not know was possible in this world. Just looking at the wind blow through the trees let me know I was not alone.

On this daily walk with God, hidden wells of secrets within me manifested themselves. As I walked with God daily, He was cutting away the callus in my heart, so I could serve Him in spirit and in truth. I was in need of a physical and emotional healing, but I was making it difficult for God to heal me because He will not impose on our will. Before the healing could take place forgiveness and forgiving were requested first, and I was willing to do both to stay in the daily presence of the Lord.

Wells of excitement leaped in me daily just to get up and walk with my beautiful God and Savior. His creation is something I have seen daily over the many years of my life, but seeing rippers on the water and leaves falling from God's view took me on a journey to forgive to be forgiven.

> *God's light is stronger than the deepest darkness. Forgive your enemies. Live as rich as you are in Jesus Christ. Are you a child of God? If not, come to Jesus. Jesus is victor. There is only one person who cannot come to Him, and that is the one who thinks he is too good to come.*
> Corrie Ten Boom

8

Take a Daily Adventure with God as you read this book, and see the things God wants to show you in your surroundings. There is no better guide than the Maker of heaven and earth, Jesus Christ.

Be blessed.

Chaper One

Invisible Things

The Lord sees everything, whether good or bad. Kind words are good medicine, but deceitful words can really hurt

(Proverbs 15:3,4 CEV)

The Word of the Lord came to me one day as I was walking from the mailbox. The Lord directed my eyes to notice one of the many trees which had been pruned earlier of its lower limbs. As I looked even closer, I noticed how the cut limbs had scabbed over and had healed themselves from the cuts. The year the trees were cut, the limbs bled with tree sap like a human wound bleeds blood when it is first cut. But to my amazement, the limbs had grown a protected cover to heal themselves.

Each pruned limb had a different type of covered scab. Some of the limbs' scabs had grown in a large rounded motion, and the others were smaller with little holes. Each pruned limb was smooth in feel other than the feel of the holes. Some had been attacked by woodpeckers and insects, but the overall tree was still tall and strong. All of the cut limbs had smooth healed scabs covering them, even the one with the insect and woodpecker holes.

As I looked closer, God spoke to me about how He can heal the wounds in my life. "All of the cuts from surgery you have had over your life I have healed. So why are you so worried about your future of unhealed wounds of doubts and fears?" My answer was that of an excuse. "I am different from the tree. I have feelings. People have misused me over the years, and I do not do not understand why." God did not let me get by with that answer. He asked me again why I could not be like the tree limbs and let Him heal me of all of my wounds spiritually, mentally, and physically. "Lord, I do not know why. I do not know why I will not let You heal me! I need Your help, Lord!"

But then, I looked at the trees again and saw them as I once was, wounded but now healed of the cuts they had acquired in their lives. They stood against the elements of the weather, spring, summer, winter, and fall. When the many elements of nature came against them, God shielded them from the attacks of the enemy. When they were wounded from the insects, He restored the damages and replaced them with a hedge of healing protection.

An unhealed wound is what happens when you are sleeping with the enemy, eating with the enemy, bathing with the enemy, driving with the enemy, talking with the enemy, weeping with the enemy, and worshipping with the enemy. The enemy will rob your life of joy and your walk with God. Unforeseen problems and worries will leave many wounds exposed and, God cannot heal them because we are too sick from the whining of life to feel His touch. Living with the enemy will turn your life into a **what, rather than an answer to your healing and daily walk with the Lord.**

As I looked at the trees again, I realized my house (body) was a party hall estate. I was having a daily pity party. The sad thing about my pity party was, I was having it with the enemy of sorrow. I thought I had a strong faith in Jesus. Was I fooling myself? I am thankful the glorious and blessed Lord Jesus gave me another chance to get it right this time. I could have left this life one frightening but blessed night when I stopped breathing, without knowing the full beauty of living for the Lord, as He commands us to do.

With joy and a peace of mind, I now look at the trees as reminders of the healing power of God. The pruned limbs are my reminder of how God healed my blood pressure. I was required to stay on bed rest a whole year. My pressure stayed so high that I was on two to three pressure pills a day. Still my pressure was out of control. Pain was and is my constant companion. But guess what? The closer I get to God the easier my pain is to bear.

My whining is no more. **My pity party is now a prayer gathering. Joy is my makeup. Thanksgiving replaced my whining. Prayer is my daily pill. Healing scriptures are my daily clothing. Belief in the power of God is my covering. Joining my husband's hands in prayer is my battering ram against the enemy.** But most importantly, pleading the blood of Jesus daily washes me clean and keeps me covered from Satan's attacks.

Through my daily walk with God, I have learned to depend on Him completely. Looking at the many things in nature as I walk each morning has restored my faith in the Lord Almighty. Not that I did not have a true belief in God, but I was failing to use the power Jesus gave us, His children, at the cross. I was letting the enemy have control of my live. I was letting the whining take the place of my joy. I was looking to man for my answers rather than God. I was going to the doctors for the medicine I needed rather than the Supplier of healing which is His Word.

The butterfly is an ugly caterpillar before it changes into something beautiful. It will not always be ugly. Beauty is right around the corner. Hold firm to the 7000 promises of the Lord, found in His Word. Let the ugliness of worries turn into something beautiful-Power and Love of God.

God bless you as you read MY DAILY ADVENTURES WITH GOD.

CHAPTER TWO

Potato Vines, Yellow Leaf on the Tree and Muddy Rubber Boot

The Lord God gives me the right words to encourage the weary. Each morning he awakens me eager to learn his teaching. He made me willing to listen and not rebel or run away

(Isaiah 50:4-5)

On this dazzling day I am thankful the Lord has shown me so many things I needed to know in order to heal and grow in His grace. With each one revealed, I could see with thankfulness what the Lord wanted me to see. The dazzling morning greeted me with a cool and windy breeze on my face. The coolness from the breeze gently dried the sweat from my face as I walked about looking at God's beautiful creation. Walking in the midst of God's beauty brings a peace I have never felt before. The morning worship amidst the glorious works of God seems to put me in a spiritual realm I have never been in before.

As I walked to my vegetable garden, I saw tiny vines growing vibrantly from the sweet potatoes that John, my husband, dug four weeks before. Then I saw potatoes the rain had washed up that were hidden under the soil. While looking at a potato, it brought to mind how we try to hide undesirable things from others. As I looked at the top of the potato, I whispered, "Thank You, Lord, for revealing this to me." Looking even closer, I began to think how often we try to hide things even from God, the One Who knows everything. We think when we are by ourselves and no one is looking that it is perfectly acceptable to do our own thing apart from God.

Mercifully, another "Thank You, Lord" was whispered again. "Lord, forgive me for my wrongs and my hidden secrets. But, Lord there are no hidden secrets from You." Looking at the unearthed potato once more, I knew sooner or later all of our so-called secrets will be revealed; exposed for all to see what was once covered under the sickening soil of deception. Our secrets will be seen as if we are naked standing in a shower covered with soap. But the soap will not wash the sins away. There will be no one able to give us a towel to cover ourselves from the view of God. Only God's blood will be able to wash us clean. And He will be the only One who can hide us from the enemy in the cleft of His hands once we ask forgiveness.

Next to the potatoes were small vines growing from some of the covered potatoes which were left. "Thank You, Lord, again for showing me my wrongs, fears, and worries," I murmur. Vines were growing from the potatoes without any roots. It does not take much to grow a vine. A long-stemmed potato cannot be used to cook or bake with, but it can grow a vine. I knew then the potatoes would not be able to produce any more potatoes without good healthty soil and strong deep roots. Deep calls to deep in the roar of your waterfalls; all your wave and breakers have swept over me (Psalm 42:7).

Still other seed fell on good soil. It came up, grew and produced a crop, multiplying thirty, sixty, or even a hundred times.

(Mark 4:8)

Once again, God revealed to me that I must be rooted in His soil to see heaven. I looked closer and some of the vines were dying and drying up because they were growing on top of the ground. I looked across the row and saw vines John missed when he was digging some weeks before. The vines were still growing and running over into another row. The potato vines were rooted and had good soil in which to still grow. There were still good potatoes under those vines that could be eaten. They were still producing good fruits. Once again, I wanted to be rooted in the True Vine. I want to please the Father and Creator of the true garden, with the fruit I am bearing.

I am the true vine, and my Father is the gardener. He cuts off every branch in me that bears no fruit, while every branch that does bear fruit He prunes so that it will be even more fruitful. You are already clean because of the word I have spoken to you. Remain in me, and I will remain in you. No branch can bear fruit by itself; it must remain in the vine. Neither can you bear fruit unless you remain in me (John 15:1-4).

Father, I do not want any secrets in my life, or do anything that is not pleasing to You. I want my vines to bear good fruit for You, Lord. Father, let me be rooted in You, so I will see Your face when my vine is pruned forever. Thank You for revealing my short-comings', and giving me a chance to be a rooted vine. I ask for Your forgiveness. Amen.

17

Later on into the morning, the Lord still had something more for me to see. As John and I were sitting at the table eating breakfast, I noticed one yellow leaf among the many green leaves on the maple tree. The leaf stood out bright and shiny among the others. It was also the smallest one hanging among the other leaves. I kept looking at the leaf as it was moving with the breeze. The Lord began to unfold what He wanted me to see. Like the other leaves, it was moving in harmony as one family. The green leaves were in harmony with the little yellow one. They all moved together in the wind. Not one of the leaves tried to push it aside or hide from it. The yellow leaf was protected from the wind because the green ones had it surrounded.

The yellow one added beauty to the others. The colors all blended together well. It was similar to a pretty fall color dress swaying in the soft breeze. It also looked like a baby being sheltered by its parents and the community. The leaf was a member of a mighty tree that was rooted in good soil. The tree could take the furies of the wind and sun. It could take the forces of the insects that attacked it during the summer months. The tree was strong enough to hold all of the leaves. The tree was the mother to all the leaves.

My train of thought was broken when John asked me what I was looking at through the window. "A yellow leaf," I answered. As he looked at it, I asked what it reminded him of hanging there. He asked me what I meant by that. I said, "The one yellow leaf among all the green ones is revealing God's command for the changing of the seasons". "What does it mean to you?" I asked. "It reminds me of hatred." "Hatred?" "Yes, look at the yellow leaf. It is hanging among all the others leaves. There is no "Who is this?", and "Why are you here?" You cannot play with us because you do not live in this part of town." The leaves were hanging together on the same tree, the tree God made, the tree that is giving life to all the leaves. There is only one tree; the leaves know they cannot live apart from each other if they wanted to remain strong and able to survive. The tree is the leaves' source of life and they are of one family, 'The Maple Family'. There is one mother and one father for all the leaves, big or small, yellow or green.

Likewise we, as human beings who recognize God as our Father through Christ Jesus are of one family-the family of God. He is our source of life. Apart from Him we will die eternally. This is also an example of the way God wants all of His children to live, in harmony with one another. As one tree with many leaves of all kinds, He is the tree which gives us life. God wants us to live in harmony with each other, surrounding the ones who are weaker-to be a shield for the ones without shelter. God wants us to be a mother or father to the parentless. When we fall, there should be someone there to catch us. Also, God created each one of us to work together so we can fit together like a puzzle.

Her ways are pleasant ways, and all her paths are peace.
She is a tree of life to those who embrace her; those who
lay hold of her will be blessed.
                                                           (Proverbs 3:17-18)

Father, let me be like the leaf, willing to live and love others as You command. Amen.

As time moved on, God still wanted me to learn another lesson from the day. When I went out to the garden to pick mustard greens for dinner, the ground was still wet and muddy from the rain a few days earlier. I wore my rubber boots so my shoes would not get the sticky mud on them. As I walked up and down the rows to get the biggest leaf mustard in the garden, the mud covered my boots like a scab on a sore.

The mud was so sticky it caused my feet to get stuck in the muddy tracks I was making. The more I walked, the more the mud stuck. When I finished picking the mustard greens, I stepped out of the muddy garden and went to the water hose to clean my boots. The closer I came to the water hose, the harder it became for me to walk. The boots were trying to come off my feet because the mud was weighting them down. As I walked, I curled my toes in the boots to try to keep them on my feet. When I finally got to the water hose and began to wash my boots, the mud did not want to come off. I kept turning my feet to get to the sticky part of the mud, but the mud still did not want to come off.

As I washed the mud off, the Lord revealed another lesson to me. The mud was an example of how we try to hold on to the sins in our lives. God washed away our sins with His blood, but we still hold on to things He wants us to let go of in life. The more He washes our sin, the harder we try to hold on to what He washed away.

I looked at the muddy boot again, and the mud was still hanging on the sole of my boot. I washed some more, but the mud still stuck. Instantly I said "Lord help me not to hold on to the things that are not pleasing to You. Lord, I give You the fears I carry around.

Father, forgive me.

Help me to become free of them.

I am the Lord, the one who encourages you. Why are you afraid of mere humans? They dry up and die like grass. I spread out the heavens and laid foundations for the earth. But you have forgotten me, your Lord and Creator. All day long you were afraid of those who were angry and hope to abuse you. Where are they now?
(Isaiah 51:12-13, CEV)

Which of you by taking thought can add one cubit unto his stature?
(Matthew 6:27)

20

The sleepless nights I did not turn to You for my rest. Father, forgive me. When thou liest down, thou shalt not be afraid: yea, thou shalt lie down, and thy sleep shall be sweet.

(Proverbs 3:24)

The times I am troubled and cannot forgive the ones who have harmed me. Father, forgive me.

For thy Name's sake, O Lord, pardon mine iniquity; for it is great.

(Psalm 25:11).

When I worry about what others think of me, Father, forgive me. Heaviness in the heart of man maketh it scoop: but a good word maketh it glad.

(Proverbs 12:25)

For the times I do not want to give of my talents You have given me. Father, forgive me. But he that had received one went and digged in the earth, and hid his lord's money.

(Matthew 25:18)

For the times I did not turn to You for my answer, Father, forgive me. Thy word is a lamp unto my feet, and a light unto my path.

(Psalm 119:105)

For the times I did not get on my knees to pray as You commanded, Father, forgive me. The Lord hath heard my supplication; the Lord will receive my prayer.

(Psalm 6:9)

For the times I did not give You, and for not giving praises for my blessings, Father, forgive me. Think upon me, my God, for good, according to all that I have done for this people.

(Nehemiah 5:19)

21

...the twenty-four elders fall down before him who sits on the throne, and worship him who lives for ever and ever. They lay their crowns before the throne and say: "You are worthy, our Lord and God, to receive glory and honor and power, for you created all things, and by your will they were created and have their being."

(Revelation 4:10-11)

For the times I looked to man rather than You, Father, forgive me.

Thou shalt have no other gods before me.

(Deuteronomy 5:7)

You are in for trouble if you go to Egypt for help,. or if you depend on an army of chariots or a powerful cavalry. Instead you should depend on and trust the holy Lord God of Israel.

(Isaiah 31:1, CEV)

Father, I ask for Your mercy and forgiveness.

But now being made free from sin, and become servants to God, yet have your fruit until holiness, and the end everlasting life.

(Romans 6:22)

For if you forgive man when they sin against you, your heavenly father will also forgive you.

(Matthew 6:14)

God will bless you, if you do not give up when your faith is being tested. He will reward you.

(James 1:12, CEV).

Father, Jesus Christ, thank You for Your forgiveness and mercy. Thank You for giving me a chance once again to thank You. I am sorry for my shortcomings. Father, I know in You nothing is impossible. Hear and receive my prayer in Your Name. Amen.

CHAPTER THREE

Lightning and Rainbow

Father, this is another glorious day You have so lovingly blessed me to see. I thank You. Thank You for waking me this morning to see a day I have never seen before. Father, I thank You. Use me and guide me where You would have me to go. Point me in the right direction so the way that I walk will be pleasing to You, Lord Jesus Christ. Father, keep my heart from thinking the things that are not pleasing to You. Keep my eyes from the things that would cause me to falter. Shield my ears from hearing the things that would cause me to stumble. These are blessing I am asking in Your Name. Amen.

The phone rings, "Hello." "The students are having a fit over the rainbow. It is so pretty! I know you might not be able to see it because of all the trees around you. But it is so pretty!" says my friend. I get up with the phone to my ear staggering to the back door to see this wonderful and exciting rainbow I was awakening from a sound sleep to see. "I do not see anything!" I answer.

"OK. I just wanted you to see how pretty it is," my friend says.

Since I was awake, I went outside to see if I could see this rainbow from a different view. To my surprise, the rainbow was over my head. How pretty the sky was. The colors were orange with a light glow of mist.

I hurried back into the house to get my camera to take pictures of the lovely colored sky. I began to shoot the rainbow from many directions. I shot it overhead. I took it with the trees in the pictures. I took it with the house in the picture. I walked farther in the yard and took it from the south so I could get the full rainbow which, of course, was impossible.

Lord, what do you want me to see and learn today? This is now my daily question to God. Lord, what do You want me to see in this glorious morning sky?

As I walked in the yard, I looked to the east and saw the bright glare of the sun. It was so bright that my eyes could not look into it. But, it cast a glow on the clouds in the west which was glorious to look upon. The color was wonderfully bright. I looked overhead and saw the rainbow with its many colors. I looked to the west and saw clouds in the western sky. Then a few drops of rain began to fall. I looked up at all the beautiful things in the sky, and the many things that were taking place over and around me.

A loud clap of thunder began to rumble. Then I saw lightning in the west. I began to think how in the world is all of this going on with the sun shining, and a glorious rainbow in the sky.. The rain poured even harder and harder. I walked fast from the paper box where I had ended up during my wandering. The thunder got louder and louder. The lightning got stronger. I was thinking to

24

myself, I better get in the house quick with all this thundering and lightning going on.

I walked in the house with my cameras covered under my shirt. Then I went to the window and looked out at the many sights in the sky. Lord, I see what You want me to see.

The radiance of God is too bright for man's eyes to see. The sun is my ray of hope when I am troubled. God is always with me in the midst of storms. I am a child of the light. In the storms of life God has me covered with His light when the world of darkness tries to come against me.

For the Lord God is a sun and shield; the Lord bestows favor and honor; no good thing does he withhold from those whose walk is blameless. O Lord Almighty, blessed is the man who trusts in you.

(Psalm 84: 11-12)

The sun will no more be your light by day, nor will the brightness of the moonshine on you, for the Lord will be your everlasting light, and your God will be your glory.

(Isaiah: 60:19)

The rainbow covered the sky with glorious color as far as the eyes could see. I looked and looked but I never saw the end of it. God's love for us extends farther than the eyes, heart, and mind can conceive. His love is never-ending. God put His rainbow as His everlasting covenant for His people.

This is the sign of the covenant I am making between me and you and every living creature with you, a covenant for all generations to come: I have set my rainbow in the clouds, and it will be the sign of the covenant between me and the earth. Whenever I bring clouds over the earth and the rainbow appears in the clouds. I will remember

25

my covenant between me and you and all living creatures of every kind. Never again will the water become a flood to destroy all life. Whenever the rainbow appears in the clouds, I will see it and remember the everlasting covenant between God and all living creatures of every kind on the earth.

(Genesis 9:12-16)

The sound of the thunder reminded me of Heaven's thunder John heard while on the island of Patmos.

From the throne came flashes of lightning, rumblings and peals of thunder.

(Revelation 4:5)

Then I heard what sounded like a great multitude, like the roar of rushing water and like loud peals of thunder, shouting:

"Hallelujah!

For our Lord God Almighty reigns. Let us rejoice and be glad and give him glory!

(Revelation 19:6-7)

Then in my spirit I could hear the Lord telling me what each meant. I could understand what God had shown me this wonderful day. "I am your Light when your path seems dark. I am your everlasting covenant. When people misuse you look only to Me. I always keep My promise. You are My child now and forever. Then I knew the meaning of each:

- The Sun – I am the light before you, in you, around you, and between you and the darkness.

- The Rainbow – My love has no end. Wherever you go I have you covered with My precious blood.

- The Thunder – Keep the faith because I am with you in good and bad times, even, when you cannot hear Me. I bring the rain to wash and cleanse you."

CHAPTER FOUR

Falling Leaves

Lord, Jesus Christ, thank You for this another glorious and beautiful day. Thank You for the lovely sounds of the birds singing in the trees. Thank You, Lord for giving me the love for Your great and mighty creation. Father, I ask you humbly again, show me what You want me to see today. These Your blessings in Your Name. Amen.

"Thank You," is all I could say when God revealed the leaves falling from the trees. Each leaf was falling in a graceful and flowing way. As each flowed to the ground, I said to myself, "What gentle beauty God has created." As I sat and watched, my husband was still in the house, so I was able to watch without any interruptions. I was still in deep thought of the leaves falling when my eyes fell on the clock in the truck. Then I began thinking that we were going to be late for my dentist appointment.

In God's amazing and creative way, He brought my attention back to the leaves falling. I did not have to ask again what He wanted me to see. God quickly turned my attention to the tree from which the leaves were falling gracefully.

As I watched the leaves fluttering in the cool moist air, I then realized this was the way our worries should fall. I looked at the tree and it was big and strong, but the leaves were still falling from it. It did not try to catch the leaves. It just stood there with its limbs gently moving with the wind.

Then God revealed to me that the tree needed rest from the long season with the leaves attached. The weight of the leaves on the trees was being removed so the tree could get its much needed rest. The leaves were also falling to ease the tree of the burden and heaviness of them.

I looked even closer at the tree and the falling leaves. The Lord once again revealed to me. This is the way I want you and all My children to let go of your worries and fears. Let everything fall from you like the leaves from the trees. Do not take them with you. Let them lay where they fall. I will fight your battles.

I looked at the tree. Most of the leaves were flowing gently in the air before they hit the ground. The ground was covered. The ground was covered with the many colors of the fallen leaves, and I could feel my many colors of troubles lighten as I watched. The ground was similar to a warm and colorful winter blanket on a cold day; my heart was warming from the display of love God was showing me.

I began to think how the grandchildren were going to enjoy jumping into the leaves when they came for the weekend. Then I thought how my husband was going to rake them all into a pile to feed the garden for the coming spring. Also, I envisioned the sounds of the ruffling of the leaves as I walked in them each day.

Watching those falling leaves, I knew right then how God was preparing me to go to the dentist. I have had a fear of dentists for a few years. I hated to go because of a bad experience I had some years before. I let my fear and worries drop off like the leaves. And to the dentist office I went with confidence and joy. I stood still like the tree and let God catch all my fears and worries. When I got in the dentist's chair, I felt no pain. He finished filling a cavity in record time.

Like the tree, I was due for a rest from my fears. I stood still and God fought my battle.

For ye shall not go out with haste, nor go by flight: for the Lord will go before you; and the God of Israel will be your reward.
(Isaiah 52:12)

Not only were all my fears falling like the leaves, but God had provided fun for the grandchildren when they came for the weekend. He gave food for the garden and the lawn. I had a calm and relaxing day after I left the dentist's office. Walking in the leaves brought a joyful sound to my ears.

How wonderful it is to have a Father who knows all of our fears before we do. God knew I was worried about going to the dentist, and He prepared for me to watch the falling of the leaves to calm my fears.

Oh, what a wonderful and loving Father I have in my Lord and Savior Jesus Christ. Thank You, Lord, for giving me the needed answers to my many whining and complaining questions.

1. What do you do when you cannot comb your hair?

2. What do you do when you turn all night in pain?

3. What do you do when you are confined to complete bed rest for a year?

4. What do you do when you cannot speak above a whisper? And if you do, it feels as if your head may explode.

5. What do you do when each year you may be facing surgery?

6. What do you do when you have to eat a two- and- half-pound hamburger badly cooked?

7. What do you do when you have never held your newborn grandchild?

8. What do you do when you see a person you love so dearly work all day and then come home to bathe you, wash the clothes, mop the floors, wash the dishes, and has to eat most of his meals out?

9. What do you do when you see the person you would give your life for not be able to touch you because he is afraid he may cause you more pain?

10. What do you do when you see your weight constantly going up when you never eat a full meal at a time?

11. What do you do when your loved one comes in from a long church meeting and cannot wake you up?

Thinking of these many things and seeing God's dazzling works added a peace I needed to calm my fears. Be still and know He is God. To be like the tree, and to depend on God for the answers was worth going to the dentist.

CHAPTER FIVE

God's Shelter

All kinds of birds will find shelter under the tree, and they will rest in the shade of its branches.
(Ezekiel 17:23 CEV)

Thank You, Lord Jesus Christ, for keeping me safe last night while I slumbered in my warm bed. Thank You for waking me this morning to see another magnificent day. Father, keep me through this day. Look over my family as they travel on the highways to and from their jobs. Father, keep and protect my friends as they journey through this day. Open my eyes to see all You have for me to see this day. Father, hear and receive my humble prayer. In Your Name I pray. Amen.

What a marvelous and fabulous day the Lord woke me to this morning! As I sat in my bathroom, the light from the morning sun shone through the window with a drizzling glow. I put on my clothes as fast as I could in order to go outside to see the sky better.

As I walked in the yard, my eyes were drawn to the loveliness of the morning sky. The clouds were reddish pink in color just like the ones I saw in my dreams the night before. I could not believe what my eyes were seeing. Or, should I say, my eyes were taken to a vision God had shown me during the night.

When I looked to the north, the sky was covered lightly with bluish clouds. I could see the blue cloud revealing a cloud that was white and beautifully shaped. I say, "Lord what is this You want me to see?" I turned my head for a moment to look in a different direction, and when I looked back to see the white cloud, it was gone. "Lord, what do You want me to see?"

I walked a little farther in the yard. And then another cloud caught my attention. It was pinkish. The white cloud was slowly parting itself so the pink color could be seen. It was shimmering with a reddish glow. As the cloud parted, the shimmering red was shining through. "Is this what you want me to see, Lord?" I said. God still did not reveal to me what He wanted me to see in those beautiful clouds. So I walked on.

While I walked, I noticed the reddish clouds shining through a large old tree. I walked farther in the yard to get a better view, but a large tree was blocking the view. I walked onto the porch to see the clouds better. That effort failed. I went a little farther on the porch, but trying to see the clouds from the porch failed also. I leaned over the porch rails to see. To no avail. I looked at the tree and all its branches. The branches shielded the house and anything standing under it from all view of the sky.

I looked closer at the tree and its charm. It was big with branches that protected and shaded the house from the direct sun. It protected anything that stood under it, near it, or in it from the sun's rays and weather. It had served as a clothesline when I was growing up. It had been hit by lightning, and recovered from the damage. It is a home for the squirrels. It is a shelter for the birds. It keeps the soil from washing away from the lawn. It provides shade in the summer and blocked the cold wind in the winter. The birds take refuge in it in the spring until their young are able to fly. When there was danger the birds hid in the arms of the limbs.

The breeze is cool in the summer. It is a music hall for the animals and birds to sing their lovely melodies. This tree covered over half of the house. The limbs reached out many feet in all directions, and as long as you stand under those limbs the sun never touches your skin. This tree shielded my family from the elements long before I was born.

Now, I understand Lord. Looking at that tree made me realize how God is our refuge when we call. He shields us from the dangers of life. He fights our battles. He provides refuge in the storm. He gives us the cool breeze when the heat of the world is too hot to bear. He is our music when we cannot hear anything else. He covers us with His love when we think things are hopeless. His loving protection reaches farther than we deserve. He is our shade from the hatred of the world. He blocks the stones of the evil one. He keeps the world from washing our blessings away. He takes care of our children when they are away from us.

When we are faced with danger, He is our arm of protection and He will hide us. He shields us from all the things life brings our way. The Lord never leaves us. We leave Him, and then we become His enemy (Romans 5:10).

As long as I am His child, God is my tree of shelter. I can run to Him because He is my tree of protection. God is a tree that never will fall. He is a tree that never fails to answer when I call. When I am down, He will carry me to His highest limb, and nothing can touch me. When I am sick He heals me. When I am sad, He put music in my ear to calm my stress. Now Lord, I know what you wanted me to see today. You used the tree to shelter and protect the animals, and to give shade to us from the sun. I know when I turn to You, God, You are much more than the tree. You are my Savior and Shelter.

CHAPTER SIX

Have Not Fear

But you will not leave in haste or go in flight; for the Lord will go before you, the God of Israel will be your rear guard.

(Isaiah 52:12)

The Lord is my light and my salvation, whom shall I fear? The Lord is the strength of my life; of whom shall I be afraid?

(Psalm 27:1).

How many times have you mislaid something and you look and look trying to use your little know how to find it? The Lord tells you to wait. Be still (Psalm 46:10a). He will fight our battles. It is God's job to see the unforeseen in our path and to guard us from it. Each day there is something new that the Lord shows me. Yesterday was no different, and it was amazing the way everything happened.

THE KEYS

John misplaced his keys Sunday morning when he was picking up the morning paper. When he was getting ready to leave for church, he could not find his truck keys. He looked for awhile but then decided he would use my set, so he would not be late for Sunday school.

After he got home from church, he retraced his steps looking for those keys everywhere he thought he had walked during the morning. He looked through all his suit coats. I wondered why when he only wore one Sunday morning! He got the flashlight and walked in the yard and driveway looking for those keys. He looked in his closet and, by the way, ended up cleaning and throwing away some junk. He went back to the church and looked for those keys with no luck. He kept looking and looking. He looked for four days with no luck in finding those keys.

By the way, we do not go on luck. We go on faith. Faith is something he did have because he did not give up on finding his keys. But there was one thing John forgot to ask for, and that was for the Lord to guide him to the keys. Yesterday, when he asked the Lord to give him sight so he could see the keys, guess what? God did!

When John was carrying the garbage cans to the road something amazing happen. The Holy Spirit told him to look down on the ground and to his left, and to his surprise, the keys were laying there. We had walked, driven, skipped, spit, and mowed over those keys for four days. God kept them from our sight until John asked for His help.

The job of God's angels is to fight for us, God's children. Our job is to trust. Be still, and God will handle finding any keys you and I have misplaced. Those keys can come in the form of any worries we are carrying around. And the key is to look to God for our help. He is the key to every problem we may be facing. Do not let the keys to your problems be hidden from your sight.

Father, thank You for Your guiding light when we cannot see our way clear. Let us be humble enough to know we cannot do anything apart from You. Keep us humble so You can use us to see Your glory and power when Your light seems hidden from us. Hear and receive this prayer of Your humble and thankful servant. Amen.

Fear is the unlocked doors of our worries.

F = False – Hopes are false when we depend on luck rather than the One who holds the key to every door.

E = Evidence – Our lack of faith is evidence when we look to man to unlock the hidden doors of our lives.

A = Appearing – The enemy can make the good things from God appear bad.

R = Real – All of our problems seem real when we do not look to the One who controls our future.

And Samuel called the people together unto the Lord to Mizpeh; And said unto the children of Israel, Thus saith the Lord God of Israel, I brought up Israel out of Egypt, and delivered you out of the hand of the Egyptians, and out of the hand of all kingdoms, and of them that oppressed you: and ye have this day rejected your God, who himself saved you out of all your adversities and your tribulations; and ye have said unto him, nay, but set a king over us. Now therefore present yourselves before the Lord by your tribes, and by your thousands.
(1 Samuel 10:17-19)

39

CHAPTER SEVEN

Poll Day

Great peace have they which love thy law: and nothing shall offend them.

(Psalm 119:165)

Today is an exciting day for the ones planning to go to the poll to vote. I am getting ready to work as a poll holder. I enjoy looking at the faces of all the people who come in to vote. I also like hearing the discussions of the ones they think are best for the job. Listening to the many comments the voters make is amazing.

Some complain about what the candidates are not doing, but they vote for that candidate again. Some complain they should have stayed at home because none of them (candidates) are doing anything, but they end up voting.. Some complain that there is no difference in the candidates, but vote. At the end of the day, the one they complained about the most has the leading vote.

With all of the complaints I hear each time I work, I am still excited about working. I am getting up earlier than usual this morning so I will be on time to hear all the different gripes people will have. Believe it or not, I am overjoyed to see new and old faces and the opportunity to serve my fellowman despite their grumbling.

I got up about 5:00 a.m. to see what the Lord wanted to show me this morning. I opened the shades to the bathroom window to look out at the clouds which were giving rain on this Election Day. As you can tell, the bathroom is one of my favorite rooms in the house. I do my best reading and meditation there. This room gives me the privacy I need. The bathroom is the room everyone stays away from, just in case something personal is taking place.

This day is just as beautiful as all the other days because the Lord made it. The sky is an unusual bluish gray because of the rain. The hibiscus has pretty pink blooms with green leaves surrounding them. Raindrops are hanging from the tips of the surrounding blooms. The pretty blooms can be seen clearly in the rain from the window. The flower stood high with blooms lifted high as if pointing to heaven. The rain is falling heavily on the blooms, but they are standing calm and not moving or bending from the large heavy raindrops.

The trees are swaying with the rain and warm breeze. With each movement of the trees branches, I can see the rain shimmering in the light. The leaves are falling as if they are dancing in an early daylight musical. The leaves are falling with one landing on top of another. The ground is flickering with an adornment of wet color of fall leaves.

The birds are flying from one tree to another. They are singing as if they are in a bird quartet. The birds are in a playful movement of activity with one bird swooping down on another bird's back. Then the second bird flies lower to dodge its advances. Some of the birds are twisting about as if they are dancing while in flight. What a creative sight to take in before facing unhappy voters.

I went into the kitchen to make coffee and to put some breakfast on for John and me. But, before I could start the pot, I went to the kitchen window to look out again. I still needed to know what the Lord wanted me to see today. Nothing was revealed.

I went back to the bathroom to finish dressing for the day. While I was there, I looked out the bathroom window again. I looked at the flower still standing tall and straight still looking to heaven. The trees were still swaying in the breeze. The birds were still flying and singing. The rain was still falling. The clouds were still giving out rain. The leaves were still dancing as they fell to the ground.

Now, I knew what God was showing me. Even with the election going on, and people worrying about who would be the next president, nothing in nature stopped doing what God had designed it to do. Everything in nature was still performing and obeying God's command. The rain was still watering the earth. The leaves were still falling to feed and warm the ground for the winter. The birds were flying freely as the Lord commanded them to do. Nothing stopped because of the election.

The Lord let me see some of the things He created doing their jobs. No worries. No "What I am going to do?" No "Who is the best man?" They know God is the One who supplies all their needs, the One who cannot be swayed by what people think. But He can give us what we need. He is the One who keeps things in balance. He is the One who controls the wind and rain. He is the One who lets the leaves change their color. He is the One who woke me and every other thing in nature this morning. He is the One who woke all of the complaining voters. He is the One who gives them the voice to complain. I left home with a smile on my face, and joy in my heart.

I went to the poll happy to be able to see and know that the One who is in control of the rain controls my life. He is the One who keeps the flowers standing tall and strong in the heavy rain. He lets the birds sing their praises. I did not worry who was going to win the election because I was surrounded with the greatest Winner of all, the Lord Jesus Christ. He won the battle at the cross so I would have a chance to be saved. He won a battle for me to have a life after death. He won the battle of death, and has the key to lock up Satan. I am the child of a Winner. He won at the cross so I can stand and say I am not afraid of tomorrow. He won the battle at the cross so I can say I am the child of a Mighty King.

So, I went to the poll and told all who would listen, that I was not worried about who won this election. These are the things God showed me today. I already knew these things, but needed a reminder that I had nothing to fear.

I left the polls happy that I had a chance to see some of my old students, to see them grown and productive, to see them doing some of the things I once taught them in class. I left knowing that I had a chance to be a witness for the Lord to tell someone to put their trust in the Lord rather than man.

I was given the opportunity to see God working once again in my life and others. Nothing stopped or changed because the election was going on, but something better happened. I got a chance to see old faces again, and to see that my many years of teaching were not in vain. And to walk in the footsteps of my mother, who sat years doing the same thing I did at the poll. These are the things God wanted me to see this rainy but beautiful election day.

44

The best Man won on Calvary. So why worry? Satan cannot do anything apart from God, and my present and future are in God's hands.

Give us a king to lead us," this displeased Samuel; so he prayed to the Lord. And the Lord told him: "Listen to all that the people are saying to you; it is not you they have rejected, but they have rejected me as their king.
(1 Samuel 8:6-7)

Thank You, Lord, for Your great and wise ways. Thank You for the things You revealed to me this lovely day. Thank You for letting me see Your amazing hands at work once again. Thank You for letting me see students I had not seen since they left my classroom. Thank You for turning a worrisome day into a day that brought much joy to me and others. Thank You for giving me understanding of the things that I did not understand before. Father, hear and receive my prayer in Jesus' Name. Amen.

Let my cry come near before thee, O Lord: give me understanding according to thy word. Let my supplication come before thee: deliver me according to thy word. My lips shall utter praise, when thou hast taught me thy statutes. My tongue shall speak of thy word: for all thy commandments are righteousness. Let thine hand help me; for I have chosen thy precepts
(Psalm 119:169-173)

CHAPTER EIGHT

Ground Covering

Because on this day atonement will be made for you, to cleanse you. Then before the Lord, you will be clean from all your sins.

(Leviticus 16:30)

I often wonder why I like cleaning on rainy days. To be truthful, I really do know why. Everything seems so damp and nasty on these days to me. When the rain comes I feel as if I need to clean all the grit and grime I see surrounding me.

As I looked out this morning, the rain was falling lightly, but still too hard for my daily walk. I got my glass cleaner and wax and started to clean. I went from room to room dusting and cleaning glass and furniture. I changed my bed and cleaned the nightstand next to it. I went to my den and cleaned all the pictures in the room. I dusted all the tables and stands. John mopped the floors because he knows how I am about seeing dust.

After I finished cleaning, I began to cook breakfast. Then I put on dinner and sat and read some of the paper. But before I could finish it, I saw something else I needed to do. I noticed that one of the pictures was crooked on the wall, so I fixed it. Why do I do this? I thought to myself. Before I could answer myself,

47

I went to the phone and called John's Aunt Mary who was having trouble with her leg. I talked to her for a few minutes, and then I started to think of something else I needed to do.

I got the phone again and called to check on another friend of mine who had been having headaches. I told her I needed to clean my nasty house. She reminded me that my house was not nasty and that I just wanted to do something. As I was talking to her, I noticed the ground was covered with wet leaves. They were all around my side door. I looked at the leaves for awhile and kept talking to my friend.

I sat in my chair after my phone call ended and just looked at the rain fall. I just looked and looked. The rain kept falling. The leaves were just laying there. Nothing was moving. The sound of the rain was peaceful and calm. I got up to do something else. Why? I had cleaned the house. I had cooked. But what time have I given to God this day? I prayed when I got up. I prayed before I ate breakfast. I prayed when I asked what He wanted me to see this day. Then it was revealed to me. "How can I show you what I want you to see today if you will not be still to listen."

Then a great and powerful wind tore the mountains apart and shattered the rocks before the Lord, but the Lord was not in the wind. After the wind there was an earthquake, but the Lord was not in the earthquake. After the earthquake came a fire, but the Lord was not in the fire. And after the fire came a gentle whisper.
(1 King 19:11b-12)

I was cleaning the house, but God wanted my heart to be just as clean. He wanted me to be calm like the sound of the rain that was falling. He wanted me to be still like the leaves lying still on the ground. He wanted me to see with eyes washed clean like the pictures I was cleaning. He wanted me to be fired up for Him like the stove cooking the food. He wanted me to read His words and eat it like the food I was cooking. He wanted me to be busy for Him, like when I cannot wait to clean the house. He wanted me to shake the dust from my ears so I could hear, and clean the dust from my eyes so I could see Him better.

Still my journey for the day carried me to see more leaves which had made a path for me to walk on. I was waiting for John to come to the car when I noticed how the leaves had made a path to walk on to the garden. As I looked at the leaves, I notice the spot that was covered was once a bare spot in the yard. Usually, I had to walk around the garage to get to the garden when it was raining. When it is wet, the mud gets on my shoes and makes dirty tracks in my clean house. But this day, the leaves made a walking path to get to the garden without me getting muddy.

When I looked at the leaves, I knew God was making a dry and smooth path for me to walk on. My feet did not get muddy when I walked on the leaves. My shoes remained dry and clean. The path the Lord makes for me in life is smooth and safe if I walk in the way He wants me to walk. The path He makes will carry me safely through life. The path He makes will not let my feet get stuck in the filthy parts of life.

I have refrained my feet from every evil way, that I might keep thy word. I have not departed from thy judgments: for thou hast taught me. How sweet are thy words unto my taste! Yea, sweeter than honey to my mouth! Through thy precepts I get understanding: therefore I hate every false way.
(Psalm 119:101-104)

The path God makes will keep my shoes clean so I will not make grimy tracks that will cause my heart to be unclean. The path He makes will not let me carry around the uncertainties of the world. God prepared a path that will lead me to do His will. The leaves were the path to the garden, but God paved the way for me to follow to the garden of the saints.

You will seek me and find me when you seek me with all your heart.

(Jeremiah 29:13)

And you, my son Solomon, acknowledge the God of your father, and serve him with wholehearted devotion and with a willing mind, for the Lord searches every heart and understands every motive behind the thoughts. If you seek him, he will be found by you; but if you forsake him he will reject you forever.

(1 Chronicles 28:9)

The good hand of our God is on everyone who looks to him, but his great anger is against all who forsake him.

(Ezra 8:22)

Thank You, Lord, for showing me the hidden and covered secrets of my heart, and for giving me the understanding and wisdom to correct them. The mud symbolized the sins we let stick to us in our daily walk. But even with a muddy path of deception facing us, God provides a safer way. The clean floor is the only path to heaven. When the sins of life come Jesus' blood washes and cleanses us from life's trash. "Keep cleaning, My child, but let it be the house which houses Me, the Holy Spirit."

Chapter Nine

Wandering

I have seen something else under the sun: The race is not to the swift or the battle to the strong, nor does food come to the wise or wealth to the brilliant or favor to the learned; but time and chance happen to them all.

(Ecclesiastes 9:11)

Beautiful clouds and a gentle wind met me at the door as I walked out this morning. Fall is in the air. This is the first time this season the fall temperatures were felt in the air. The coolness, softly touched my arms as I walked in the yard. I walked to the back to see the night rain on the newly- grown rye grass John had sowed two weeks before. The sight of the green grass was an enjoyable sight to my eyes.

The pond beneath the backyard fence was sparkling. Looking at the water in the pond brought back childhood memories of fishing with my grandmother.

My grandmother went fishing on this same pond when I was a child. After she would finish her breakfast dishes, all of her grandchildren would follow her to the pond. She had her own special can seat to sit on. No one else was allowed to sit on it when she was around. She would bait her hook, spit on it and fish. We would listen to her tell us stories of the old days, and we would spit chocolate pretending it was snuff. She would fish until it was time to fix lunch for my grandfather, and afterward would go fishing again until it was time for us to milk the cows. What memories!

The fish were making beautiful waves in the water. The bugs were flying from one stem of grass to the next. I was overjoyed with the many sights my eyes were envisioning, and the many memories of my childhood. I went back in the house to get my camera because I knew the Lord had something special to show me this day on my morning walk with John.

Before John and I started on our morning walk, I asked the Lord what He wanted me to see. Nothing was revealed to me, so we started out on the path we normally take.

I looked at the clouds, but nothing was revealed. I looked at the trees. Nothing was revealed. I looked at the trash John was picking up along the way. Nothing was revealed. So we walked and talked along the way. We got to our turning point, but we decided we would walk a little farther than we usually walked because it was a wonderful morning.

John put down his trash buckets and we went down the hill almost at a jogging pace. But before we got halfway down the hill, something hit us in the face. It was raining. When we left, the clouds were almost breaking. The sun was trying to break through. I had taken a picture of the breaking clouds a half mile back. We could not believe it was raining on us that quickly.

We turned around and walked as fast as we could, but we were too far from home to beat the rain. So we slowed down and had a morning walk in the rain. The rain was hitting us in the face. The mist was cool, but refreshing. The most amazing thing of all, was that the rain was falling but our clothes did not get wet. My hair and face were wet, but not my clothes. The rain was cool, but we did not get cold. The rain did not spoil our walk; it cleaned our face and hair. It was one of the best walks we had had all week.

During the leisure walk, I began to think how we are sometimes deceived. Things look one way, but it is not what it seems. Looking at the sky we could see the sun trying to break through, but it soon faded away. It also showed me how God takes something that is meant for bad and turns it into something good. We enjoyed the morning walk in the rain as much as we enjoy walking in the dryness of the day.

The wicked have laid a snare for me: yet I erred not from thy precepts.

(Psalm 119:110)

I learned a most valuable lesson when the deceiver comes against us, God will not let him touch us no matter how many obstacles he throws in our way. When our names are dragged through the mud, it won't halt us. When the storms of life are raging, we will not be touched. When we are lied about, the truth will be revealed before it lays a hand on us. God can cover us from the dangers of life. He may let it rain on us, but we will not get wet with things of the world when we are under God's protection.

Father, thank You for the gentle rain on my face this blessed morning. And for protecting my path as I walked through the day. Thank You for showering Your pure and gentle love over me and all Your children as we walk this journey of life. Amen.

CHAPTER TEN

Living My Own Words

Heavenly Father, I want to thank You for giving me the will to live what I speak. Today is disappointing to me, but I remember Your Word. Fear not because I am always with You. Thank You, Father, for walking with me today and all the days when I am feeling down. You are my strength and guide. I know I can do nothing without You, and nothing can be done against me because You are my shield in the times of storms.

Father, forgive me for worrying when I know You take care of me when I do not know where to turn. Father, thank You for these many blessings in Jesus' Name I pray. Amen.

I got up this morning feeling fine. I had a great night's sleep. The first cool night of Fall helped me to sleep like a baby (a sleeping baby). I did not want to get up because the weather was cool, just the way I like. The phone began to ring early this morning, so I knew it was time to get up. When the phone starts to ring it seems as if it rings until I get out of bed.

The ringing of the phone reminds me of how my father's voice sounded, high and piercing to the ears. He would call for me when I was a child to get up early in the morning on the first cool day of Fall to gather firewood. The bed was warm and soft, and the sleep was good. How I hated to move from my cozy spot.

When my siblings and I were small, my father would also come and open the curtains so the light would shine in our faces. Now that I am older I realize the importance of having an earthly father who kept me in the light, as well as having a heavenly Father, who is the Light. Then he would say, "It is time to get up. There are more chores to do." There are many chores to do also for the Kingdom of God. How I hated to move from the bed again because it was so warm and secure. God is the warm protection. It felt as if nothing could touch or harm me there. In God's arms I am safe from the terrors of this world. The covers were soft and warm. My spot, as I called it, was warm from a deep night sleep. I am the apple of God's eye, so there are no worries of losing my place. The heat from my sisters' bodies was like an electric blanket. The Lord is the supplier of our needs. I was in bed heaven. Then all at once, the covers would fly back and a stringing on the legs. When I stray from the Word of God, the devil has a chance to harm me. "I told you to get up," my father would say. "There are cows to milk and chickens to feed." There are souls to be fed. I would roll out of a heavenly cushioned haven to a cold morning of chores: milking cows, feeding chickens, carrying wood for the wood heater, only to name a few. To work for the Kingdom of God is hard sometime, but who will go if not I?

Slowly, I rolled out of bed to a cool morning of adventures with God. I walked slowly to the bathroom to dress (in the armor) and then out the door I walked. The cool and windy air touched my face, and childhood memories crept in again. I walked the yard with a childlike heart. And God said:

> *I tell you the truth, unless you change and become like little children, you will never enter the kingdom of heaven.*

(Matthew 18:3)

Lord what am I to see today? I walked on to the pond where I fished as a child, but nothing was revealed. I walked the hills of the yard and watched the birds soar high in the sky. Nothing was revealed. I looked at the pecan tree with all its leaves lying around it on the ground. Nothing was revealed. I walked in the house I was raised in, and looked at some of the things from my childhood. Nothing was revealed. I watered the plants, and pulled off all the dead leaves. Nothing was revealed. Well, Lord, I guess I have a day off, I thought to myself.

John and I left for our morning walk. The sky was blue and the Fall smells of burning leaves and coffee perking were welcoming. We walked and talked about nothing of importance to anyone else but us. John picked up the trash that was thrown out during the night. A car came by and the driver stopped to talk. We talked for a few minutes and he drove off. Then we heard the sound of another car. It stopped. It was the mailman. He knows John and I from walking each day. He gave us the mail. Thank you was given to him for not letting us wait until we got home to get it.

I opened the letter that I felt was of importance. To my disappointment, it was somewhat disappointing to me. I slowly read as I walked. I would stop at times to understand better what I was reading. Then I walked faster to get into the house so I could make a phone call. I thought what I was reading was a mistake.

57

But it was not. I began to whine. I cannot believe this. I whined some more. I made another call. I still did not feel any better. So I whined some more.

All at once, I thought about all the things I say to other people about faith and trust. You cannot let things get you down when they do not turn out like you think. God has another blessing for you. Now, I can give out good advice, but I was doing the same thing I had been telling others not to do. The night before, I said the same words to my daughter, "You have got to look to God because He can handle any problem." Now, the shoes are on my feet. Turn to God. He can handle any problem.

Now, Lord, I know what You wanted me to see and learn this morning. MYSELF. "How can I bless you if you keep whining?" God seemingly whispered.

Thank You, Lord, for showing me myself this morning. It is so easy to give advice to others, but when we are wearing the shoes we become blind. Thank You for letting me see me, And letting me understand again that You can handle any problem I have. Thank You for not leaving me when I whine. Amen.

Chapter Eleven

A Cup of Coffee

Father, Lord Jesus Christ, thank You for letting me have this valuable time with my grandchildren. Thank You for the innocence they bring into the house. Thank You for the pure joy they bring in their talk and smiles. Father, take care of my family today in our comings and goings. These are the blessings I am asking in Your Name I pray. Amen.

During the summer our grandchildren come for the summer months. John and I enjoy having them in the house. There is never a moment without something unusual happening. Lil' Derrell always says something unusual and funny. We can never let him see us laugh at the things he says, because he will keep it up until he becomes tiring. Our other grandchild Za is always mature and sensible about the things he says. He also will lie if he thinks he can get by with it.

John and I never can walk early in the morning when they are here. They sleep later than we do, and the sun is too hot when they get up. I take my morning walk outside to see the many things God has to show me. As usual, I ask the Lord what He wants me to see for the day.

On this day, I did not see what the Lord wanted me to see when I went out. I walked in the yard as I do each morning, but nothing was revealed. I looked at the ants, working. There was a trail of them working as if they were on an assembly line. One line was going, and the other was coming. The ants in the line that was going did not have anything on their backs. The ones coming back were weighted down with something white. I looked down, and they had some crumbs that were lying on the walk. I hated to disturb the working of the ants. But what I hated more was for them to bite me. I called John, so he could put some ant bait on their trail. Within a few minutes the ants were going.

I came back into the house and busied myself like the ants. I put on some coffee. I turned the oven on to cook breakfast, and I set the table for breakfast. I always try to have breakfast on the table before the boys got up. I love to see the boys' eyes when they get up and the food is greeting their senses..

I started to fix the things the boys like to eat. I made one of Lil Derrell's favorites and one of Za's. I put on the kettle to heat the water for their hot chocolate. I cut up the apples and oranges to put on the table. After they got up, John helped them to get dressed for the day. After they dressed they came to the table for breakfast.

"Woo whew, Grandmamma, I like this breakfast!" Lil' Derrell said. "Thank you," was my reply. The food was blessed, and we began to eat. "Grandmamma! Can we have some coffee? We like coffee!" Lil' Derrell said. I got up and fixed two cups of coffee and returned to the table. We began to eat. The boys said how they loved the food, and how they loved the way I cook. They were afraid I might not cook any more for the day, so they were buttering me up.

Lil' Derrell kept telling me how he loved the breakfast. As he neared the end of the meal, he started to drink his coffee. "Grand-mamma, this coffee is burning my heart. Grandmamma, this coffee is too hot because my heart is burning."

I held back my laughter. He was full and did not want to drink the coffee. I said, "Okay, do not drink anymore coffee, because I do not want your heart to burn."

I looked at the face of a child that could not think of any other way to keep from drinking coffee, than it is burning my heart. We cleared the dishes from the table and all the dishes were washed. Then the boys went out to ride their bikes.

Later on that day, I began to think how we burn the Lord's heart over the things we do when we try to keep from doing the things He commands us to do. We make excuses to keep from giving our tithes. We are stealing from the Lord, and that burns His heart. We do not love our neighbors as ourselves. It burns God's heart. We do not forgive when someone misuses us. It burns God's heart. We do not turn the other cheek. It burns God's heart. Every time we disobey, God's heart burns.

After lunch, we cleaned the table and washed the dishes. The boys went out to ride their bikes. As the boys were riding, I went to the front porch to watch them as they rode. I watched as each one went up and down the hill. They rode on the sidewalk and in the grass. A few minutes later, my nephew came over to play. His bike was not working. He asked Za if he could ride his bike. Za told him, no. He told him he was not going to let him ride his bike because it was his. My nephew called my name and said, "Za will not let me ride his bike. And that ain't fair. He is being mean to me." I sat for a moment without saying anything.

Earlier in the spring, my nephew had a new bike. He was letting everyone ride it. Two or three boys were riding it at one time. I called his grandmother and told her that he was going to tear up his bike the way he was riding it. And then he would not have one to ride. Even though I told her about the boys riding the bike, it did not stop. The bike was torn up before spring was over.

Do I make Za share his bike which he has taken care of since the day he got it three years ago? Should I let my nephew tear up something that was taken care of for so long? I sat and thought for awhile, and then I asked Za if he would let him ride for awhile.

They played together most of the day. They played ball and John took them fishing. Afterwards, I fed them a snack. They ate and talked about fishing and playing ball. They talked about video games. They talked about who played the best game. They talked without complaining.

I looked at each one of them and said, "Yes, Lord, we must come as a child." If I had not let my nephew ride the bike and complained about how I told him he was going to tear it up, he would have left feeling bitter. If the Lord would remind me of all the things I knew I should not have done, I would be in trouble. I looked beyond my nephew's faults and saw his needs; just as the Lord looked beyond my faults and saw my needs, before I was wise enough to come to Him. How blessed it is to see through a child's eyes. My heart burns when I see God's innocent child misused.

CHAPTER TWELVE

Visitors

Lord, thank You for waking me this morning. Thank You for the lovely sunshine this morning and for giving me another chance to look upon its loveliness. Thank You for protecting my children as they travel the busy highways and freeways. Thank You for putting a shield of protection around and about them. Father guide and protect us through this day. These are the blessings I am asking in Your Name. Amen

The soup is boiling over, and the phone is ringing. I woke to a cool and crisp morning. The sun is shining bright and throwing off a beautiful cast of rays through the trees. The birds are flying high in the sky. They are so high it seems as if they are disappearing in the sky. Only a small spot can be seen of them. The grass is wet from the light night fog. The flowers are still looking up to the sky. As I was looking at the many things God was showing me, I lifted my hand to heaven to give my praises for such a wonderful Savior – a Savior, who woke me this morning. A Savior who protected me through the night. A Savior who has all power in His hands. A Savior who shows me mercy when I do not deserve it. My hands were lifted in thanks and honor. Lord, I thank You for being so kind to me, and Lord what do You want me to see this glorious day? Nothing was revealed.

As I walked in the house the phone was ringing. John answered with excitement. "How are you doing today? It is nice hearing from you! Yes, we are home. No, I was not here last night, but my wife was. Oh, you have a chance to come by, but it is nice talking to you." This was a friend, who had come to town. He had gone by to see all his friends except John and me. But he wanted to call before he left town. He had gone to the house across from us the night before, but he did not come by to see us.

Some months before, we had helped him to sell some of his property. During that time he called mostly every day. He came by to see us when he came to town. He stopped by to see us before he left town. I mentioned to John, how people will come to visit when they need your help. They are your best friends when they need you to do something for them. I shared how sometimes I feel bad about the way people use me when they have no other place to turn.

However, God did not let me feel sorry for long. He reminded me that I sometimes come to Him when I am in need. How I sometimes forget who woke me in the morning. Who kept me safe through the night, and who kept me as I was walking among His Creation. He reminded me that I am supposed to trust Him completely. He reminded me how sometimes I do not stop by the altar to see Him there; I just call when I have time. He reminded me of how I call Him in my spare time. He reminded me that He never whines and complains about my shortcomings. So I cut some more potatoes to make soup for whomever today.

CHAPTER THIRTEEN

Morning Duel

Father, Lord Jesus Christ, thank You for the morning light You woke me with this beautiful and blessed day. Thank You for keeping me through the night. Thank You for keeping and protecting my family and neighbors. Amen.

"What a morning!" I said as I looked out the bathroom windows. I did not have time to ask the Lord what He wanted me to see. There were two birds prancing at each other. One was blocking the other. When one bird tried to move, the other bird would block it. The two birds strutted the length of the storage building. I laid my head in the window and laughed at the sight.

One of the birds that was being blocked flew upon the roof of the house, and the other bird flew on the roof of the storage building. They watched each other from their positions. The bird that flew on the house flew back to the place that it was blocked from. When it flew back down, the other bird flew back down and strutted in front of it again. It hopped in front of it each time it moved. If it moved to the left, the other bird followed in front of it. If it moved to the right the other bird moved the same way. If it moved to the front the other bird stopped it. Their heads were upright with their beaks straight up.

The blocked bird flew up on the roof again. The protected bird turned its head to see where the other had gone. It was as if it was trying to fool the other bird. When the protected bird's head was turned, the other bird flew back to the same spot that it was blocked from. The protected bird turned and saw the other bird, and it blocked it again. The bird would go one way and the other bird would stop it. The bird blocked the other one all the way into the yard. I stood there watching until I could not see the birds any longer. I was afraid to move because I thought they would hear me and fly away. After a few minutes, the birds were back in sight again. They pranced around the flower. They pranced around one side then the other. They went a little farther in the yard. The protected bird still would not let the other bird pass. Then the bird flew on the fence. The protected bird saw where the other bird had flown it flew after it. They went completely out of my sight, so I left the window.

Lord, what do you want me to see? The birds are prancing after each other. What do You want me to learn from this? I could hear the Lord telling me, "This is how I protect you." My angels stand in front of you so nothing can harm you. When evil comes against you, they are there to keep it from passing. They never sleep and are always on watch. I am with you always- when you are up and   when you are down. When things seem to high to reach, I am with you. My eyes are always on you.

Dust

I hate to see dust, and I hate dusting, but I like the end results. I like the way the furniture looks when it shines after using furniture polish. The smell is so nice and fresh. When you walk into the house the smell meets you there. It is not loud or too strong.

It is just enough to lend the scent of cleanliness. I find myself dusting as soon as I see the furniture with the least bit of dust on it.

The sound of the cloth on the mirrors and glass tables give off a clean sound as the glass shines. I like to hear the rubbing sound of the cloth. When the glass is clean and shiny you can see your reflection in it. When the sun hits the glass it casts a glow of many rays of color. The mirror throws a reflection of a prism on the ceiling in the room. The prism of many colors seem as if they are dancing across the ceiling in harmony. The colors are dazzling. When the leaves move on the trees the prisms moves with a gracefulness only God can give. There is one thing I notice about the prisms-they do not give a reflection if the window and mirrors are not clean. If the glass is not clean there will be ugly streaks on it. The ugliness of the smudges make the whole mirror look ugly and unclean. The prisms are not clear and pretty with the smudges because the reflections are blocked.

After looking at the dust on the tables, glasses, and mirror, it's a clear reminder of how we miss seeing our blessings. We are blinded by the smudges over our eyes. We cannot see clearly because we let dust settle. The blessings of God falls on us without us sometime knowing when they are falling. But we like the end results. When we keep ourselves dusted from sin, God can enter our lives. Our true gifts will never shine like the prisms, until we clean the streaks of doubt, worry, anger, bitterness, and more bitterness from our lives.

God's beauty shines best when we are willing to receive it. All the dust and smudges in our lives must be clean and shiny like the mirrors. Our light must shine with all the beautiful rays of God so others may see Him in us.

CHAPTER FOURTEEN

Bird Feeders

I have been sitting and waiting almost all day for the Lord to show me what He wants me to see this magnificent and cool day. I got up this morning and looked out my bathroom window as usual, but the Lord did not give me anything He wanted me to write about today. John and I went for our morning walk, but nothing was revealed. I took a drive downtown but nothing was revealed. I came back and got lunch ready. Nothing was revealed.

"Well, God must want me to rest today," I said to myself. Then I thought, maybe He wants me to answer some e-mails. Sure enough I had two that needed answering. The Lord guided me to what I needed to say to each person who needed my advice. These are the words of my reply to a friend who was having marital problems:

Faith makes trouble less frightening: "Then the high priest and all his associates who were members of the party of the Sadducees, were filled with jealousy. They arrested the apostles and put them in the public jail. But during the night an angel of the Lord opened the doors of the jail and brought them out.

'Go stand in the temple courts,' he said, 'and tell the people the message of this new life.' At daybreak they entered the temple courts, as they had been told, and began to teach the people.

(Acts 5:17-21)

I do truly love him!

I DO TRULY LOVE HIM. Listen to your words. (I do truly love him!) Do you hear what you are saying? Honey, love heals. Think about what Paul says about love. The greatest of all is love. Love overcomes the things that have hurt us. Love can take the bad times and turn them into good. Now, if you have love, use it to heal and forgive. The Lord forgives us when we ask, and He forgets. If God forgives and put our sins as far as the east is from the west, why can't we?

As far as the east is from the west, so far has he removed our transgressions from us.

(Psalm 103:12)

Satan is the one who is causing you to cry. God does not do that. He gives us complete joy – joy to look to another day. Joy to hold our heads up and shake off all that has harmed us, and Joy to say I will fight to the end. It is Joy that can wipe the sad tears away and replace them with a smile that comes from the heart.

Also Satan will work through anyone to destroy God's plan. You have a family you love. Keep it.

I told you my story because I want to help you not to make you leave your family. I have forgiven my first husband because as long as I dislike him, he still controls me.

I want you to think of one thing. Is your family important enough to save? If so, stop crying and save them. Forgive your

70

husband for whatever he has done, because we all do things we shouldn't.

One more question I need to ask you. Is crying solving your problem? Tell him you forgive him, and believe me things will turn around. If you tell him, let it be from the heart. It is easier to keep a family and heal the things that are wrong, than to make another family. I was blessed, but I see so many who are not. Work as one-when it relates to love, money, children, pain, and the list goes on.

Listen to your words, and truly hear yourself..

DRESS YOUR HEART FOR GOD'S BLESSING. PUT SATAN WHERE HE BELONGS. REMEMBER SATAN BE-LONGS IN HELL, NOT YOU. GOD LOVES YOU AND SO DO I. ALSO, YOUR HUSBAND LOVES YOU. YOU CAN SEE IT IN HIS EYES. DON'T YOU KNOW THAT?

This is what God wanted me to do today. So I put on some music and sat out on the porch and rocked in the rocking chair. All at once, I heard something I thought were blackbirds coming. I got out of the chair and looked over head to see the birds. There were no birds. I looked at the blue jays flying to the ground and back to the tree. Then I noticed the bird feeders were empty. I got up to get the feed to fill them.

I filled one feeder at the garden. Then I went to the front of the house to fill the ones there. I filled one and replaced the cover. Then I went to the birds' favorite blue feeder to fill it. I filled it full to the top. When I put the cover back on, all of the seeds wasted out. I looked at the cover and discovered I did not put the inside cover that controls the flow of the seeds back on. I looked at the seeds on the ground and said, "Oh, well, the birds will eat them from the ground today."

I walked off to fill the feeder under the trees near the porch. I opened the feeder and discovered the feeder was already filled to the top. I looked at it and wondered why the seeds were not coming out for the birds to eat. I picked a stick up from the ground and stirred the seeds. I stirred them up from the bottom, and pushed the seeds down so they would go through the opening and the birds could get to the seeds. When I looked back inside the feeder I noticed the seeds had big worms crawling in them. The worms were coming to the top of the seeds. The feeder had more worms in it than seeds. The worms had hatched from the seeds of the last filling.

"Well, I understand now what You want me to do." I just had finished e-mailing a friend and telling her how the Lord wanted her to turn her worries and fears over to Him. I also had told her how the Lord could heal the hurts in her life. She e-mailed me back telling me how she had tried to turn everything over to the Lord, but one moment she felt fine and later on, she felt sad. She could not let go of the things she had been harmed by. She was also having a problem with forgiveness.

The Lord revealed to me then how His words can fall on empty ears. No matter how His words are preached or read, if we are not willing to hear them the words will not flow. Every word goes straight through like the seeds in the blue feeder. Also, anger and unforgiveness can eat us up like the worms I found in the seeds.

We must let go of the hurts in our lives so God can heal us. Anger can eat away at our salvation and the chance to see Him face to face. God wants us to be filled with His love. God does not want His words to fall on empty ears. "Look at the bird feeder and hear My words. Be not empty, but full of the things I have

72

in store for you. Have no worms in your life. Forgive those who have misused you. Forgive so you will be forgiven."

Do not say, "I'll pay you back for this wrong!" Wait for the Lord, and he will deliver you.

(Proverbs 20:22)

Father, thank You for the unseen lesson You revealed to me today. Father, help me to get the worms out of my life so I can live a life pleasing to You. Let me not be empty, but full so I can hear and receive Your words. Amen.

CHAPTER FIFTEEN

Birds Working Together

The sky is full of the different birds doing their own thing. I am having a hard time thinking wisely this morning. The birds have my attention.

When I went out earlier this morning, I greeted the day as I always do. "Good morning beautiful day. Lord, what do You want me to see this day?" Nothing was revealed. So John and I left for our morning walk as usual. The air was cool, and the breeze was pleasant to my skin. We walked and talked as we usually do. The clouds were blue with white ones passing overhead. The wind blowing in the grass and trees was slow in movement. The chill was pleasing to my face. I did not have to worry about sweating as we walked because the light wind dried it like a gentle kiss on my face.

As we were walking, I noticed how pretty the clouds were becoming. I slowed down my pace just to look up at the unusual looking clouds so I would not fall. One peculiar cloud looked like an angel in flight. As we walked, the cloud was in front of us. When we turned at the turning point, the cloud was before us. I kept looking at the cloud as we walked. I started to mention its shape to John, but I was too occupied with its beauty to speak.

Lord, this is what You want me to see today, but what do You want me to get from it? The closer we got to home the more the cloud would change in shape. Part of the cloud looked like the wings were spreading. The part of the cloud that looked like the head was shaping itself more clearly. Lord, what do I need to know about this cloud? Nothing was revealed. "If I had my camera I could get a picture of this for others to see," I thought. Still nothing was revealed. The cloud had my attention until John and I got home. When we got close to home, the cloud was disappearing in the trees. When we walked in the yard, I could not see the cloud at all. Well, Lord, I guess there was nothing for me to learn from this cloud.

I went to the garden to pick some vegetables for dinner. While I was there I noticed how the birds were flying to and fro. They were working in pairs. One would fly to a certain part of the yard and pick up something, while the other one would fly to the same spot and pick up something else. Each one would take its turn doing whatever they were doing. After awhile, the yard was completely covered with the little birds working and singing. After they flew to the ground, they walked and sang as they worked. Every once in a while some would fly up on a tree, while the others remained on the ground. They worked and sang as they walked with no concern of the things going on around them. They worked in one part of the yard until I stopped looking at them.

What a wonderful thing to be able to work in one accord with others, I was thinking to myself. Even if other birds would come to that part of the yard, the little birds kept doing their work.

76

They kept walking and flying from the ground to the trees. They were about their business of doing what God directed them to do.

God was taking care of the little birds and they knew it by the way they were walking among the others birds. I came into the house and opened my back door to see if they would move or fly away, but they kept doing what they were doing.

What a lesson I learned from those little ones. They were secure in the hands of the Lord. They worked together. There was no fighting among them. Each one had its own job to do, and did it. When it was time for the one to take what it was digging up in the yard to the tree, it took it. The ones that were doing the digging kept digging. There was no playing among them, they were simply working.

After the little birds finished doing their work in the yard, all of them flew away together. Those little birds have not been back to the yard since that morning. What an example those little ones set for me this morning. When we are working in God's Kingdom, we should work in one accord – the accord of our Lord and Savior Jesus Christ. Also, when we enter into God's house we should go with praises and thanksgiving. We should enter in His house to work in one accord to worship and praise Him. All of my worries and fears should be given to the Lord, just as the birds walked about the yard without fear of my walking near them.

CHAPTER SIXTEEN

Pure Joy

The wind is blowing gently with fall crispness. The trees are swaying and moving with the direction of the wind. The chimes are chiming, and the rain is falling silently. The birds are flying high in the sky with a faithful motion. Hammering noises are coming from next door where the repairmen are replacing house siding in the rain. The hammering rings with the flow of a musical melody. I hear God's captivating music in the air with all the sounds of His creation.

"Lord, good morning. This is a beautiful day You have made. Thank You for this rainy day. Lord, what do You want me to see this day? I believe You have already revealed it to me, but I had to ask to make sure."

Hearing God's voice in the many wonderful sounds this morning brought pure joy to my heart. God instructed the wind to make the chimes sing with His magnificent melody. The melody brought happiness to my heart. I was hearing God speak to my heart. God speaks to whomever wants to hear Him.

Everything in nature is obeying the commands of the Lord. The wind is blowing as He commanded it to blow. The trees are swaying with rhythmic movement. The birds are flying in an orderly and scenic formation. The rain is watering the earth with nutritional regime. My ears are receiving the sounds of the hammering. The trees receive the birds to house them from the rain and to take rest. Everything is obeying God. Well, everything except man. For example, last night I tossed and turned in bed worrying about something that happened hours earlier.

And why do you worry about clothes? See how the lilies of the field grow. They do not labor or spin.
(Matthew 6:28)

While I was writing, I had stopped to answer an e-mail to a friend who was having a hard time adjusting to her son's divorce:

All I can say is God knows your hurts and pains better than you do. He wants you to turn to Him, and trust Him. "Stand still and see Me work. See my power to take nothing and make it something. If I can part the Red Sea for two million of My children to walk through on DRY LAND, will I not do the same for you?" These are the words God put in my hands to type.

Everything we think is bad God turns it to good. Remember God can, and does handle all of our problems if we will only turn them over to Him. I am talking to myself as well. We are so busy trying to solve the things God has already solved. We step in and say, "Well, it should be this way." And then the mess starts. W e have taken it out of God's hands and made a pure mess of it.

Let God dry your tears. When He dries them it is fixed the way He wants it to be. Also do not worry about your husband working if he is unemployed. If you are making it, be thankful. God put him where he needs to be at this time. John has not worked since January 15, 2002. His job fired him after he was hurt on the job. He had been working there for 18years. He was awarded "Workman of the Month" many times over. After he was hurt and could not do the work of two men, they did not need his anymore. But, you know what? God used it for good. He has become even closer to the Lord. We do so many things together now. What man meant for bad, God turned it for good.

I heard the Lord speak these words to my heart, "Be still and watch Me work. Cry if you may, but let it is tears of joy. Have PURE JOY"

EYES

After I finished writing, my mind went back to seeing the birds perched on the top of the tree in the pouring rain. They were not crying about the weather. They were singing with a joyful tune. They were flying from one limb to the next. As I was looking at the birds, I lifted my hand to heaven to give thanks, and to ask forgiveness for my worrying last night over things that God has in His control. Why cannot we be more like the birds of the air – singing the praises to the One, who supplies all our needs?

Then my eyes spotted a soaring hawk. It was flying high above the trees. It was soaring so high it seemed as if it was going to disappear in the clouds. The gracefulness of its wings open wide and its glide was breathtaking. I looked as it soared higher and higher. The wings turned with a likeness of a jet when it is about to land. Higher and higher it flew. Then all at once it soared downward. It had spotted what its eyes were seeking-eyes sharp enough to see its prey from miles above and wings so graceful in flight that it put its prey at ease to deceive. Its beautiful gliding wings hid the deadly claws that take hold of its prey without warning. No danger was in sight as the hawk was soaring. The beauty of its wings in flight disguised the danger in its claws. How easily we can be caught off guard by our worries and fall prey to the deceiver.

EARS

My eyes were looking toward heaven, but instantaneously the Lord put the sounds of the chimes in my ears. They were singing with the movement of the wind. The music was calming and uplifting. The wind was on my face, but the sound was in my ear. The presence of God was as sweet as a cold glass of tea on a hot day. The worries I had when I went out were transformed into joy. The things that were worrying me seemed to disappear in the sound of the wind in the chimes. There was no wind to see but the results was heard. How sadly I was thrown off guard with the things God had taken care of without delay. I could not see God handling my so- called worries, but with the calming sounds of the chimes God was telling me everything was alright. Later on into the day, I could hear the results.

Some days it is harder to see the things God wants me to see because I am getting in His way. I am graceful and calm like the soaring hawk with my eyes looking up to heaven for my help. I have faith and take refuge in Him like the birds in the trees. I look to God. My shelter and peace is where I need to place my worries. I listen to the sounds of God's blessings because He is the Word which calms my fears. The repairmen's hammers strengthen me. With each beat of the hammer my mind is transformed to the cross. I should have no fears because God shed His blood for me on Calvary, and His blood keeps me covered. There is no harm that can come against me as long as I keep my eyes, ears, and mind fixed on Him. I am the prey of the deceiver, but God has the keys to every door and lock. So why should I fear when Jesus rose from the grave so I can be free to enjoy His glory?

CHAPTER SEVENTEEN

Angel Tree

The winds are your messengers, and flames of fire are
your servants.

(Psalm 104:4 CEV)

Seeing God's creation and what He wants me to learn from it
is easier some days than others. As soon as I looked out this
morning I could see the wonders of God's creation sending praises to heaven. One of the evergreen limbs was pointing upright to
heaven. The limbs looked like the figure of an angel. One branch
had one part that resembled the wings. The center part of the tree
resembled the full body. One part at the top resembled the head.
The parts that resembled the wings were pointing up toward the
sky.

Trees are amazing in their own way; each one has it own style
and shape. Some have leaves that fall during Autumn, some
change colors at different times during Fall, some have leaves
that never change, and some stay on the ground year- round. Others are smooth to the touch while some stick like a pin and cut
like a knife. Some need more water than others. Some grow well
in poor soil while others need rich soil. Some limbs point toward
heaven while other limbs point downward.

Trees are like humans in many ways. We come in all shapes and sizes. We fall for anything that sounds good to our ears. We change our colors (minds) for each occasion, or in order to please. We never change (positive) when Satan comes against us. We hold to God's words. We never change our minds (negative) even if it is against the teaching of God. We stay faithful to God in good and bad times. We live as a child of God. Even when times get rough we stay in the hands of the One who can make our way smooth. We do not stick or cut each other because we do not agree. We need the water (the Word) from heaven to stay strong. God's words fall on poor listening ears, just as His words fall on rich listening ears. We give all of our praises with uplifted hand to heaven in good times. In troubled times we fail to lift our hands. They remain by our sides.

Looking at the tree, it remained steadfast in its worship to God. When the wind blew through it, the tree still stood with it limbs pointed toward heaven. When the birds landed on top of it, the tip of the limbs were still pointing upward as the birds swayed with its movement.

With the many distractions the tree stayed steadfast. I looked and smiled at the wonderful sight of the tree giving reverence to its Creator. This tree was putting me to shame because I sometimes fall short of giving reverence to the One who wakes me every morning. I was also falling short of not being a witness for the One who has carried me when I could not carry myself.

I fail to give thanks to the One who moves every stumbling block that is in my path; to give honor to the One who has given me a chance to stay here until I was saved by His precious blood and baptized with the Holy Spirit; to give reverence to the One who holds the key to my present and future and grants forgiveness of my past.

I give my humble cries to the One who kept Satan from me when I was too crazy to know that I needed His protection.

All mountains and hills, fruit trees and cedars, every wild and tame animal, all reptiles and birds, come praise the Lord! Every king and every ruler, all nations on earth, every man and every woman, young people and old, come praise the Lord! All creation, come praise the name of the Lord. Praise his name alone. The glory of God is greater than heaven and earth.

(Psalm 148:9-13, CEV)

Lord, Father God, Jesus Christ, forgive me for my shortcomings. I am not worthy of Your blessing, but I am thankful You are a forgiving God. Thank You for giving me another chance to say I am sorry! Father, thank You for Your undying love and mercy. If the trees can lift their limbs in praises, Father, I know I can do even more. Father, I am lifting all of my praises and thankfulness to thee, oh, Lord. Amen.

CHAPTER EIGHTEEN

The Cloudy Airplane

Ye are the light of the world. A city that is set on an hill cannot be hid.

(Matthew 5:14)

Seeing a new day is always a blessing. Knowing the Lord has protected and watched over me another night is more than reason enough to be grateful. I am always thankful each morning when I wake to see the sunshine, the blue sky, the birds soaring through the air and the animals run from tree to tree. I see the Lord's miracles close at hand. There are many things hidden from my view when I drive the car. I know God has His protective hand about me. It is a blessing to hear the sounds of the leaves as they are falling from the trees and hitting the ground. To hear the birds as they move across the sky or to hear and speak to the people who stop my pace of walking to say a few words. To hear the bugs creeping in the grass and to hear the music from the houses we pass as we walk.

The wonderful smells of the freshness of the Fall cut grass carry the pleasant scents of the season. To smell the morning coffee perking in the coffee pots brings back memories of my childhood when I worked in the cotton fields. The whiff of the meat cooking with the aroma of fall fills the air with holiday fragrance. The exhaust smell from the cars reminds me of how wonderful life is, and God's protections from the poisons of the world.

After I finished my morning walk, God revealed the wonders of His protection. As I looked at the northern sky, the clouds were white and beautiful. An airplane was moving across the sky as if in slow motion. As the plane was moving a cloud was directly in front of it. When the plane approached the cloud, it began to disappear in the midst it. The first part of the cloud barely covered the plane. Then it went even deeper into it. The farther it got into it the less I could see. Then within a few minutes the plane was out of sight. The cloud had covered it completely.

While I watched the cloud, my mind began to think of how God covers us with His protection. He covers us when we are about to go through a storm. He covers us when the enemy is attacking us. He covers us when danger is in our path. He covers us when we do not even know we need to be covered. "Thank You, Father, for Your protection," is all my mind could think of as I watched the clouds cover the plane from my sight.

Looking at the plane was as if God was holding me in His Hands, as though His Hands were at my right hand.

I have set the Lord always before me because he is at my right hand. I shall not be moved.

(Psalm 16:8)

The hands I lift in praise.

*Hear the voice of my supplications when I cry unto thee,
when I lift up my hands toward thy holy oracle.*
(Psalm 28:2)

Lift up your hands in the sanctuary, and bless the Lord.
(Psalm 134:2)

*Let my prayer be set forth before thee as incense; and
the lifting up of my hands as the evening sacrifice.*
(Psalm 141:2)

He is the hand that calmed the sea and wind and told it to stop. The hand that holds me when I am falling is the hand that keeps me safe in the times of storms. The hand of God is like the cloud covering the plane. I am safe and in the cushion of His hands. I am covered in the padding of His arms.

As I looked closer at the clouds, I began to thank the Lord for watching over me and keeping me safe when it seemed as if I was all by myself. The plane had disappeared in the clouds but the plane had instruments that guided it in the direction it needed to go. God is our instrument in the cloudy times of life. He is my light in the tunnel of darkness. He is my light in the clouds of despair. He is my light in the stormy sea of hurt and pain. He is my instrument when everything else fails. When I am about to fall, God catches me with the softness of the clouds. I am covered in the shelter of His arms.

Father, thank You for another day. Thank You, Lord for all You have done for me. Thank You for Your clouds and all the beauty they bring. Thank You, Lord for Your arms of protection. You are the One and only true God, and I thank You for choosing me as one of Your children. Father, carry my loved ones through this day and keep Your loving hands about them. These are blessings I am asking for in Your holy and precious Name. Amen.

CHAPTER NINETEEN

Daily Job

But love ye your enemies, and do good, and lend, hoping for nothing again; and your reward shall be great, and ye shall be the children of the Highest: for he is kind unto the unthankful and to the evil.

(Luke 6:35)

Lord, thank You for the precious night's rest You blessed me with last night. Thank You for Your protection as I slept. Thank You, Lord, for waking me, my family, friends, and neighbors this wonderful and glorious morning, and for waking us to a day that only You can give. Thank You, Lord, for waking me to see a day that is beautiful in sight and sounds. Thank You for letting me see the sun shine so bright and feel the wonderful warmth on my face. Thank You, Lord, for giving me strength to take my daily walk, and to see the things You wanted me to see this morning. For all these things Lord, You have given me to see this day; You have all my thanks and praises. Father, hear and receive my prayer in Your holy Name. Amen.

The Lord blessed John and I to get up and take our daily walk. We left as usual with the two buckets and the stick we carry on our walk. But before we got out of the yard, I asked John if he thought he should carry two buckets since he picks up the trash each day. So, he decided to leave one of the buckets.

We left the yard talking as we usually do. We looked at the leaves on the trees changing to their Fall colors. The leaves were so pretty that it caused us to stop and appreciate the exquisiteness of the colors.

Before we could resume our walk, trash appeared in our sight. The trash John had picked up the day before was lying there for him to pick up again. "Why do people constantly throw litter out when they know it makes the earth look so ugly?" I asked. John never stopped picking up the thrown out trash.

We walked on farther, and there were bottles and cans lying on the side of the road. Some was thrown in the grass on the roadside. Some was thrown in the grass on the edge of the yard. "Why can't people have some pride?" I said once more. John kept picking up.

We walked until it was time for us to make our first turn. When we turned, paper, bottles, cans, and other things I did not recognize were lying on each side of the road. We made our second turn, and a man stopped and asked if we were picking up cans. He was going to give some to us. John said we weren't. I did not say anything to John. We just kept walking until we got to the church we always pass on our daily walk each morning.

The church was white and sparkling in the sunlight. The trees behind it were sparkling with their many Fall colors. While I looked at the trees, my mind left the thought of the people throwing out trash. Looking at the church, I mentioned to John how it made me think of Christmas. The windows were shining and bright. The outside wood was flickering like snow. Just looking at the whiteness of the church softened my anger. I could see Jesus Christ and His goodness in the sparkling light. I could see Jesus Christ in the colors of the leaves. I could see Jesus Christ in the rays of lights in the windows. I knew then that the Lord wanted me to see Him and not the trash on the road.

He wanted me to see and understand that Satan will never give up testing our faith just like the trash being thrown out as soon as John picks it up. Satan works the same way. When we think we are safe from his temptings, he tries something else. But Jesus revealed to me in the sparking light in the window of the church that He is the Light of this world. And He is mightier than any trash Satan throws.

John and I walked on and as we took our third turn there was more trash than on the first road. I did not let it bother me because God woke John this morning with strength and patience enough to handle the trash. God wanted me to get the trash and complaining out of my heart, and to look to Him for my strength and understanding as I walk through the things Satan will throw at me.

As I looked at the trash as we kept walking, I then understood how the enemies of God constantly try to trip up His children. Everything possible is thrown in our way to take our focus off of God. I am thankful I saw the trash this morning because God directed me to see His glory and blessing. The church was shining brightly in the midst of the ugly trash, but the beauty of God shone through brighter than a lump of coal in new fallen snow.

Thank You, Lord, for my daily walk to see the things only You can reveal.

CHAPTER TWENTY

A Light Among Darkness

For with thee is the fountain of life in thy light shall we see light.

(Psalm 36:9)

Yea, the darkness hideth not from thee; but the night shineth as the day: the darkness and the light are both alike to thee.

(Psalm 139:12)

Light is sown for the righteous, and gladness for the upright in heart.

(Psalm 97:11)

Thy word is a lamp unto my feet, and a light unto my path.

(Psalm 119:105)

Father, thank You for giving me another day. Among the clouds I can see Your light shining through. Thank You for waking me this cloudy but beautiful day. This is the day You have made for me to see Your glory and miracles once again. Thank You, Father for giving me eyes to see and ears to hear the many

95

things only You can make. Father, guide me to see and hear the things You want me to see this day. Protect and guide us through this day. Amen.

Good morning, God. Thank You for the rain early this morning. Thank You for the clouds moving swiftly overhead. Thank You for the cool breeze that is caressing my face. Thank You, Lord, for the early morning time in Your presence, and for family and friends praising Your holy Name.

Before I started this day, I had to give thanks and praise to God. The day is breezy and wet. The rain fell heavily before John and I woke up this morning. John got up and hurried to the dry cleaners before they stopped taking clothes for the day. If he did not get his clothes there before 9:00 a.m. he would not be able to get them back tomorrow. He rushed out the door.

The phone rang before I could get my clothes on. The voice on the other end wanted some advice from me. We talked a few minutes and she was fine. After we finished talking, praises were lifted to the Lord again, because the Lord had answered her prayers. She wanted to give back to the Lord what He had given her. She gave our church a much needed face lift. She donated enough money to put a breezeway over the front door. Some of the older members were complaining about getting wet as they walked out the church door, so she blessed them with a covered walkway.

After the project was finished, so much beauty was added to the church. Many were grateful; some were angry and complaining. "Why did she want to spend her money on the church?" Some asked. No reasons were needed. The Lord had blessed her and she wanted to bless His house. There was anger in the midst of beauty and giving.

After the phone call, I went to look at the raindrops on the flowers and the tree. The leaves were surrounding the trunk of the tree in brilliant colors. The leaves had the tree surrounded as if it was being decorated for Christmas. The tree looked as if it was standing among a brightly colored quilt.

After the rain, I walked on to get the morning paper. After I left the paper box, I decided to take a short walk. As I was walking something bright caught my eye. I stopped and backed up to see what was shining so brightly among the clouds. The sun was big, and seemed closer than usual. I backed up a little farther to get a better look. Sure enough the sun was shining, but it was a soft shine. My eyes could look upon it without it blinding me. Before I could move pass the trees, the clouds had covered it. What is this Lord? What do You want me to see?

Right away I knew what the Lord wanted me to see. I had just finished talking about people being angry regarding the work that was done on the church. Some were thankful, or so it seemed, and others were angry. Looking at the sun helped me to realize how Satan works undercover to try and get his plan through. The ones who were praising her about what she had done for the church were also complaining it was taking too long to finish. Thank goodness, the Lord has a way of revealing Satan's plans.

When I got back to the yard, I looked up and saw the sun again. It was not in the place where it had been. It seemed as if it had moved directly in front of me. As I looked, the glare from the sun's rays almost blinded me. I had to look away. I looked back again, and could look directly into it. Then as I looked at the clouds, they began to move and covered it again. As the clouds passed over, the sun gave out a ray that resembled an angel. It was so bright and beautiful my eyes could barley look upon it.

97

Lightning flashed from a huge cloud and lit up the whole sky with a dazzling brightness. The fiery center of the cloud was a shiny as polished metal, and in that center I saw what looked like four living creatures.
(Ezekiel 1:4b-5)

My eyes were looking in amazement at the wonderful sight of the sun. I also asked the Lord once again what He wanted me to see. Then the answer came. It does not matter how people complain about us when we are doing His will. He is our strength in the midst of the complaining. When Satan comes against us, look to God because He is the light in the dark times.

My friend needed support during the repair of the church. God gave me the words to say to her. During the time friends were talking against her and about her, God was the supplier of her needs. God's light shows up Satan whenever he tries to stop His work.

The sun soon burned away the clouds and it shined brightly the rest of the day. The work was finished at church, and all of us are dry when it rains now. My friend was covered from the whining of the unthankful church members. Because God's house was so shiny and pretty when she finished it, the complainers were ashamed to whine amidst its beauty.

CHAPTER TWENTY-ONE

In Formation

*Praise ye the Lord. Praise ye the Lord for the heavens:
praise him in the heights. Beasts, and all cattle; creeping things, and flying fowl: Let them praise the name of
the Lord: for his Name alone is excellent; his glory is
above the earth the heaven.*

(Psalm 148:1, 10, 13)

Father, thank You for this beautiful blessed day You have
awakened me to see. Thank You for showing me the things You
wanted me to see this morning. The birds are flying in a beautiful formation and singing Your songs of praises. Thank You,
Father, for Your mighty works and loving hands about me, as I
see You amidst Your creations this day. Amen.

As John and I walked this morning, a beautiful formation of
wild geese were flying overhead. The sight was breathtaking to
behold. We walked our usual path. But to see such beauty as the
wild geese flying above filled my heart with joy and peace- peace
for the wonderful works of God, peace of knowing that God is
always near-and the peace of knowing He cares for the geese. I
am much higher than they, so I know He cares for me. It fills me
with peace knowing God guides me in the path of righteousness,
and all I have to do is obey and follow. I have the peace of know-

ing that if I stray, God gives me a chance to come back to Him. I am forgiven of my sins and God forgets the things I have done as far as the east is from the west.

The Lord is compassionate, gracious, slow to anger, and abounding in love. He will not accuse, nor will He harbor His anger forever; He does not treat us as our sins deserve, or repay us according to our iniquities.

> *For as high as the heavens are above the earth, so great is his love for those who fear him; as far as the east is from the west, so far has he removed our transgressions from us.*
>
> (Psalm 103:8-12)

The geese were flying high above in a V-shape formation. The only opening was in the back of the V. The lead goose paved the way for the others to follow. Each goose played its own part in the formation. Every angle lined up in perfect formation and there were no dips in any of the sides. Whatever direction the lead goose would go, the others would follow. Where it led, the others followed knowing they were being taken in the right direction.

> *The Lord is my shepherd, I shall not be in want. He makes me lie down in green pastures, he leads me beside quiet waters, he restores my soul. He guides me in paths of righteousness for his Name's sake. Even though I walk through the valley of the shadow of death, I will fear no evil, for you are with me; your rod and your staff, they comfort me. You prepare a table before me in the presence of my enemies. You anoint my head with oil; my cup overflows. Surely goodness and love will follow me all the days of my life, and I will dwell in the house of the Lord forever.*
>
> (Psalm 23)

100

Following the lead goose seemed so easy as they flew overhead. Why is it so hard to follow the path which God directs us to follow? We have the preachers preaching the Word, but sometimes we do not receive it because our minds wander during the long sermon. We have the Sunday school teachers teaching the Word, but we do not listen. We have Bible study classes, but we do not go if it is raining, or too cold outside; however we go to the job each morning if it is raining, if the baby stayed up all night or if the weather is below zero. We go to the job. We receive the instructions given to do the work required for our job. We listen to the plans that make our workplace better. We stay late even if it is cold outside. We stop by the grocery store and pick up a few things that are needed for dinner. Excuses!

We see all of the stumbling blocks in our path, but we keep going in that direction. We know the Shepherd's voice, but we do not listen. We hear and understand the consequences for our actions, but we do not believe we will suffer the penalty for our sins. We know we are protected by the blood of Jesus, but we believe it will soil our pretty clothes. We know the cost of our non-belief, but we think our earthly money can pay the price. We know Jesus humbled Himself for our transgressions, but we believe humbleness is for weak people.

Following Jesus is like the formation of the geese. We follow because we know He leads in the right direction. We follow because He is the Shepherd who never leads us into danger. We follow because He is the head that never wrongly leads. We follow, because if we stray, He will wait until we find Him. We follow, because He catches us when we become too weak to keep up with the stronger and younger ones. We follow because he is our Light, which shines bright when we are in a dark place.

As I looked at the formation of wild geese, I noticed that when the leader flew up all of the others followed. If one strays from the formation, it loses its direction and hope of flying. It is lost forever from the population. If we lose our direction, Jesus is there to guide us. If a flock or formation of geese needs a leader, why do we think we can stray away from God our leader and survive?

The formation of the geese looked like a wall of protection for each bird- following the one each trusted. Is not it wonderful to have a God Almighty, Who we know we can trust with the life He has given us? He is the One Who gave His Son to die for our sins, the God Who gave His Son for us all and shed His blood so we can be covered and protected from the enemy. Jesus is our leader and guide. If we will follow, we will never get lost. Yes, temptation will come to our doors, but with Jesus' lead, we could overcome.

Oh, what a blessing to have a Living God who never misleads. And if one of His own gets lost, He will find him.

Suppose one of you has a hundred sheep and loses one of them. Does he not leave the ninety-nine in the open country and go after the lost sheep until he finds it?
(Luke 15:4)

102

CHAPTER TWENTY-TWO

The Father's Voice

To him the gatekeeper opens; the sheep hear his voice, and he calls his own sheep by Name and leads them out. When he has brought out all his own, he goes before them, and the sheep follow him, for they know his voice. A stranger they will not follow, but they will flee from him, for they do not know the voice of strangers.

(John 10:3-5)

This is a wonderful day the Lord has wakened me to. Last night was a great and blessed night, also. I attended a great revival, and I slept well afterward. The uplifting revival speaker was Dr. T.L. Lowery. Some of the things I have been wondering about, he helped me see more clearly. After I got home I talked to John about the things that happened. I talked to many others about hearing God's words so powerfully and clearly. I went to bed earlier than usual. I was so filled with God's words that I did not want to go to sleep, but I tried. I slept all night and woke this morning still full. I was so full I did not want to eat breakfast.

Rather than cook, I went outside. The day was beautiful. The birds were singing and some were hiding from the rain in the hedges. The leaves were falling silently on top of each other. The rain was lightly falling on the tin roof of the breezeway. The fog was breaking for the morning. The trees were receiving the raindrops with thankfulness. The limbs were hanging as if in harmony with the raindrops. The breeze was cool but pleasant as it touched my face. The flowers were still in bloom from the summer. The squirrels were running from tree to tree. The bark on the trees was changing color for the winter. Oh, what a blessed morning the Lord woke me to this day. I could hear God's voice in the sounds I heard around me. I could see God's hand in everything my eyes took in. I could feel God's presence all about me. Oh, what a day!

Not only was I hearing God's voice, but the birds seemed as if they were listening for something also. I watched as a blue jay was sitting on a limb of the apple tree. Every time it heard something its head would turn from side to side. One tree sparrow flew in the hedge when the rain began to fall. But before it flew away it seemed as if it saw the rain before it hit the tree.

I stood motionless watching the reaction of the different birds. Each breed reacted in a particular way to the rain and breezy sounds of the morning. My foot would not move from the spot I planted it on because my mind was watching in admiration and thanks to the Lord. I stood there until my ears received the sounds of a bird call from afar.

When the sound of this bird was heard some of the blackbirds in a tree in the back-yard flew off. The sound was heard again and more of the birds flew from the tree. Once again the sound was heard, and some more of the birds flew from the tree. The bird called until all the blackbirds were gone from the tree. I thought to myself, the birds know the sound of this bird's call.

My concentration was broken when all the birds were gone from the tree. How amazing it is to know and follow the voice of the one who can lead you. After all the birds were gone, the call stopped. They followed the call of one bird. They followed in confidence. They followed without delay.

With thankfulness, I praised the Lord for showing me this amazing example of how we should follow His call. The birds knew the voice of the bird that called them. We should know the voice of the Lord when He calls us. His voice is one of love and care. His voice is the One who will never lead us astray. His voice is the One who will look for the lost sheep. His voice is the One we should recognize when we hear it. His voice is not one of a stranger, but One of a Lamb who did no harm. The voice of the One who gave His blood for our sins. The One whose blood can wash us clean.

Looking at the birds flying after the voice they recognized filled my heart with the joy of knowing how God is using the simple things of nature to teach me each day. They are teaching me to trust and believe when it seems as if troubles rain everyday. For these things I give all my thanks and praise.

Father, Lord Jesus Christ, thank You for Your many and wonderful blessings. Thank You for showing me Your creation and all the blessings which flow from it. Thank You, Lord, for putting Your sounds of joy in my ears. And Lord, thank You, for giving me a chance to see the daily things You want me to see. Thank You for giving me a chance to have a daily adventure with You. Father, hear and receive my prayer, in Your Name. Amen.

CHAPTER TWENTY-THREE

Wash Day

What a great morning! It is rainy and just the right coolness in the air. The rain is falling heavily. You can hear it falling calmly on the housetop. Everything seems so still and quiet. There are no birds singing, no crickets cricking, no dogs howling-everything is still. Even I slept later this morning. The bed felt so warm and comforting. The warmth of the covers made me feel secure. Once again, the warm blanket carried me back to the memories of my childhood. I felt as if nothing could harm me. I was surrounded with the pure and strong protection only God could give.

I slowly and hesitantly rolled out of bed. The phone had started to ring. I walked to the back door to look out at the rain falling rapidly and heavily on the ground. The rain was running downhill in a smooth and sweeping manner. The water from the rain was crystal-like and clean in appearance. Lord, what do You want me to see this rainy and wet morning? Right away God revealed the message in the rain water to me.

Clean, bathe, sponge down, swab, shampoo-these were the reminders the sight of the rain water brought to mind. The vision was that of the Lord washing away our sins. The rain water was flowing downhill and disappearing into the pond as it got to the bottom of the hill. The ground was sparkling in beauty. The sight was that of a clean and freshly washed baby. It was sweet smelling, and the sound was calm and serene. The rain water also washed the rocks clean in the ditches. As the water washed over the rocks, everything seemed to become so colorful and spotless. The water looked cool and clear. The rocks amazingly changed back to their natural colors. Some were white, some were brown, and some were speckled in color. Everything my eyes fell on seemed to be scrubbed clean of all the unwanted debris that was stuck on them. They were cleansed clean and freed of all of their extra dirt and grime of the soil baggage.

Watching the water making everthing so clean, it was an example to me of how God forgives our sins. He forgives and forgets the things we ask forgiveness for. We are cleansed from that sin not by water, but with Jesus' blood. He washes our sins away and places them as far as the east is from the west. It is also a reminder of how forgiveness is given to the lowest and most vile of us if we would only believe and repent.

> *But why do you let that Jezebel who calls herself a prophet mislead my dear servants into Cross-denying, self-indulging religion? I gave her a chance to change her ways, but she has no intention of giving up a career in the god-business.*
> (Revelation 2:20, 21, The Message)

God washes our sins away with His blood as the rain water was washing the ground of all its impurities. He washes us clean like the rain was washing the rocks back to their natural color. He washes us clean until we smell as clean as a newborn baby. He washes us clean and carries the uncleanness away like the rain water carries the dust down the hill. He washes us so clean that our sins are no longer visible in God's sight.

Chapter Twenty-Four

Dusting

Then came Peter to him, and said, Lord, how oft shall my brother sin against me, and I forgive him? Till seven times? Jesus saith unto him, I say not unto thee, Until seven times: but, Until seventy times seven.
(Matthew 18:21-22)

How wonderful it is to know God has complete control of our lives. Also it is wonderful to understand that we cannot do anything apart from His wishes. I am saying all of this so that you, the readers, can understand how God directs our paths. If, yes, if, we are willing to obey God.

All of my mornings begin with me giving all my thanks and adoration to the Lord for another blessed morning. I also thank the Lord for bringing me through another night of peaceful rest. I thank Him for watching over me while I slept in His arms of protection. Furthermore, I thank Him for protecting my family and friends while they slept in the safely of their beds. Most of all, I have to give my thanks for a day I have never seen before, and for the health and strength which only God my Father can furnish.

As soon as I finished with my prayer of thanks and praises I went to the bathroom to look at the many things God had provided for me to see. The wind was very high during the night; it woke me from my sleep. I can thankfully say I only stayed awake for a short time. Then the rain began to fall heavily, and it woke me again. Only for awhile, I am grateful to say. I went back to sleep and slept as soundly and comfortably as a baby in its mother's arms. I was resting peacefully in the arms of the Lord when the high wind woke me again, but I was not afraid because God had me wrapped in His arms of safety. I woke rejoicing with the morning light and the coolness of the morning breeze.

I looked at the many things God was showing me. I saw the fresh fallen leaves surrounding the trees. I saw the trees with most of the Fall leaves gone. The trees were in motion with the wind's movement. I saw the birds flying in the morning light. The sun was hidden under the clouds. I saw the white fence washed clean and shining from the night's rain. I saw the vegetables swaying in musical time with the gentle breeze. I saw the ladybugs clinging to the ceiling in my dining room. I saw different types of birds playing in the same tree in harmony. The Lord let me see the many things He was waiting to show me this cloudy morning in His own sacred way.

Lord, I see the many things You have shown me, but what do You want me to learn from them this morning? The night rain and the strong wind came to mind. The wind had shaken most of the leaves from the trees. It was time for the trees to have their long-awaited rest. I looked at the trees moving in the breeze. As I looked, I could see some of the leaves still falling to the ground. I looked at John and said, "It seems as if God is rocking the trees asleep in His arms like a mother rocks her baby. It is time for the

110

trees to rest for the season. God is telling the trees to go to sleep. It seemed as if He was saying, "You have worked well all year, so it is time to rest for awhile." It is so warm for this time of year, but the trees know it is time for the leaves to change, even thought the temperature feels like spring. The leaves know to fall off without hesitation, isn't that wonderful?" I knew this was what God wanted me to see for the day. So I decided I would begin to write about my daily adventures with God after I cooked my Thanksgiving dinner.

As I was cooking dinner, I thought about my mother's house and how it needed to be dusted. I asked John if he would call our nephew, Derrick, to see if he would come and dust the house. He came right away. He knew what I wanted done, and where to find all the cleaners and paper towels. I told him I was depending on him doing a good job and taking his time while he was dusting. I did not want anything broken because of getting in a hurry then I said, "Oh, wait a minute, I am not going to talk to you like a child. I am going to talk to you like an employee. You know what I expect from you, so do your job well. If you do not, I am not going to pay you."

I went back to my cooking. I cooked all the things my daughter wanted for the Thanksgiving meal. After I finished, John came into the house and told me to come and see if the house was dusted the way I wanted it. My nephew was left to work by himself, because John had to do some work outside.

When I walked into the house, my eyes fell on the things which were wrong. I looked at the piano and the dusting towel was lying there. I could see dust on the piano. Everything that was moved was where he moved it. I did not say anything. I put the things back in place. I walked to the den, and I could see dust.

The mirrors and pictures were dusty. I went in the hall and the dresser was dusty. The pictures on it were dusty. I went into the front bedroom and I could see dust. I went into the back bedroom and I could see dust. I went in the middle bedroom, and I could see dust.

I called my nephew. "What have you been doing all this time?" "I have been dusting," he said. I got the dusting towels and began to go over the places he had cleaned. When I put the towel on the spots he had dusted, dust got on the towel. Everywhere I put the towel dust showed up.

I looked at him and said, "You have not done anything in here! If I would have wanted to clean myself I would not have called you to come. I could have cleaned this house myself. I now have to go back over what you have messed up. Here I am going back over all the places you have been. I do not have time for this half doing! You just go home! I am not going to pay you for making this mess!" I was so upset and disappointed because I had to go back and clean all the rooms. I had to get them clean for my sisters and niece who were coming in for the weekend.

My nephew went out and sat on the front porch awhile, and then came back into the house. I looked up at him and said, "Why are you here?" "Just thought I would visit for awhile." "I do not need any visitors. You have just made a mess in here," I replied.

But forasmuch as he has not to pay, his lord commanded him to be sold, and his wife, and children, and all that he had, and payment to be made. The servant therefore fell down, and worshipped him, saying, Lord, have patience with me, and I will pay thee all. Then the lord of that servant was moved with compassion, and loosed him, and forgave him the debt. But the same servant went out, and found one of his fellowservants, which owed him, and took him by the throat, saying, Pay me that thou owest. And his fellowservant fell down at his feet, and besought him, saying, Have patience with me, and I will pay thee all. And he would not: but went and cast him into prison, till he should pay the debt. So when his fellowservants saw what was done, they were very sorry, and came and told unto their lord all that was done. Then his lord, after that he had called him said unto him, O thou wicked servant, I forgave thee all that debt, because thou desiredst me: Shouldest not thou also have had compassion on thy fellowservant, even as I had pity on thee? And his lord was wroth, and delivered him to the tormentors, till he should pay all that was due unto him. So likewise shall my heavenly Father do also unto you, if ye from your hearts forgive not every one his brother their trespasses.

(Matthew 18:25-35)

I dusted and fussed. I swept and fussed. I cleaned mirrors and pictures and fussed. I cleaned the kitchen counters and fussed. I cleaned the kitchen table and fussed. I cleaned the microwave and fussed. I let the blinds back down and fussed. I fussed. And fussed. And fussed. I fussed.

I went in the family room to write down my thoughts for the day, but my hands would not type the things I wanted to type. My thoughts would not come together. I tried again. My thoughts still would not come together. I tried again. My thoughts were scattered. Everything I typed sounded poorly prepared. My thoughts were mixed up. My thoughts were silly. Each sentence was odd. "What is wrong with me to day? Are my words leaving me? Is this the only thing You want me to write today Lord? God, do You want me to write today at all? In all probability, is this book finished? But, Lord, I want others to know the daily walk I take with

113

You, Father. I want others to know how You guide me daily on the path You want me to walk on. I want others to know Who gives me the sight to see the most wonderful works of Your hands, which only You, Lord can reveal daily. I want others to know that I cannot put down these words apart from You, Lord. Lord, maybe there is nothing else You want me to see. Maybe, Lord, You do not want me to write about Your arms surrounding the trees. Perhaps I am not the right person to write about Your blessings and grace in my life. Lord do not give up on me. Show me the words I should write. Father, Lord Jesus Christ, humble me so You can use me."

I got up, turned off the computer, and went back to my house. John and I were sitting at the table eating when God revealed to me how disappointed He was with me. As we were talking about the things of the day, my mind fell on my nephew, Derrick. I knew God was not pleased with me being so hasty and harsh with him. I still feel sad about it even right now as I write. Tears are welling up in my eyes as I write. I am thinking about how he probably felt, and how sad he must be feeling also. I did not pay him because I told him in the beginning I would not pay him if he did not clean the way I wanted him to. That was not right! I am thinking about how sad God feels when I mess up. And I messed up when I was so rude to my nephew. I could have said everything in a better way. I could have handled everything in a calmer and more godly way.

I understand how the tears fill God's eyes when He sees me going about with dust on me and in my eyes. The dust of worries and fears, the dust of unkindness, the dust of anger the dust of misunderstanding and the dust of not being an example of His love and patience. I understand that God is not hasty or harsh with me when I fail to live up to His words. I also understand how bad God feels when I keep letting the dust of the world blind me from Him. I understand how God feels when I cannot see my true self in the mirror, because the dust on me keeps getting on the mirror so I am unable to see things clearly. How often has God followed me to clean up the things I mess up and cannot handle without Him? God gives me the instructions to follow, but I have to follow them. I know if God paid me according to how well I work, I would be fired and lost. I know now that God constantly gives me a second chance, so why was I so harsh with Derrick?

Now, I know what God wanted me to see once again, myself. I called my nephew to come back today. I did not get an answer at his house. While John and I were eating our Thanksgiving dinner, Derrick came and sat with us and ate fried turkey.

He knows how much we love him. We paid him for some of the work he did yesterday and everything was forgiven just as God forgives us.

Father, when I started to write on the things You had shown me this day, my ideas would not flow as they usually do. I understand why, and I want to thank You for showing me myself once again. Father, keep me humble so You can use me to do Your will. Father, forgive me for my shortcoming. Let me be an example of Your love and blessings. These are my words asking for Your forgiveness. Hear my prayer, Father, in Jesus' Name. Amen.

CHAPTER TWENTY-FIVE

Holding On

For if the first fruit be holy, the lump is also holy: and if the root be holy, so are the branches. And if some of the branches be broken off, and thou, being a wild olive tree, wert graffed in among them, and with them partakest of the root and fatness of the olive tree.

(Romans 11:16-17)

It appears as if it is getting more difficult to see what God wants me to see each day. Or is it me forgetting to let Him guide me? Sometimes I might be too eager to see. Sometimes it might be that I am taking God for granted. I might be me thinking He should just let me see what He wants me to see as soon as I get out of bed without His direction. But, now, I have realized that I am too quick to see, what I want to see, rather than wait on what God will show me. It is so easy to take God for granted. Lord, let me apologize now. Lord, I am asking for Your forgiveness once again. Teach me to be patient.

Yes, the Lord has taught me to wait on Him. He taught me when He did not let me see His works today with understanding. Over the last few days God has shown me who's in control. And believe me, it is not me. I went to and fro all day without God revealing anything to me. I walked to get the paper as I always do in the morning. I did not feel that God was showing me any-thing I had not seen on previous days. I went back to get the mail from the box, and I still did not feel anything. Lord, what do You want me to see? I did not hear or see anything. I went to my mother's house to do some work there, and I still did not feel any-thing. I turned on some soft music so I could think better. Still nothing was revealed.

My thoughts were of sadness, because I had not heard from the Lord. I felt once again that it must be time to end these daily adventures with Him. I felt that all the lessons He wanted to teach me had already been revealed.

I went to the computer to make some Christmas cards for my aunt. When I turned on the computer, I notice I had forgotten to bring my card disk with me so I left the house to come home to get the disk and pictures. Before I got past the front walk, the Lord directed my eyes to the very center of a large scrota bark (nut) tree. My head turned all the way back so I could see well. The leaves were all off the tree, but near the very center top of the tree was another small tree growing from it. The tiny limbs were still covered with green leaves. What an amazing sight I thought to myself. What in the world is that little tree doing there? I was walking and trying to look at the same time. After I came back to the house my eyes still searched for answers.

What Lord, do You want me to see? Is there a lesson in this tiny tree? Still nothing was revealed. Nothing special came to me, so I went back to my work.

After I finished making my cards, I closed up the house and came back to my house. I came in and fixed a plate for myself. I sat down and began to eat. Well, there will not be any writing today, I was thinking to myself.

Darkness was falling and I started to close the blinds for the night. As I was closing the blinds, my eyes noticed a very large and beautiful light. The moon was shining through the trees. The moon was so big and bright it looked as if it was in a movie. "What a wonderful sight!" I said aloud. I got my camera out and went outside to take a picture of the beautiful moon.

The night was passing and still God had not given me anything to learn from on this day...or so I thought. I went to the computer so I could check my e-mail. I got them all checked, and still nothing was revealed so I sat and watched at a special on T.V.

The night is almost gone and it is time for me to go to bed for the night. My book is coming to a close, were my thought. I went to the bedroom and got my clothes ready so I could take my bath. I laid back in the bathtub and sang praises to the Lord for a wonderful day. I sang songs of old. I sang songs my mother and father used to sing. Something came over me and I started to praise and thank the Lord more and more. I just thanked Him over and over again.

God reminded me of the baptism of the Holy Spirit I received a week ago tonight. Then He revealed to me the tiny tree growing into the big one. He revealed to me how I was trying to hold on to the old me, but He had given me a new me. The tiny tree was the new me. New life. New growth in Him. The tiny tree was growing when all the other leaves had fallen off and dried up. The tiny tree with the green leaves was God's way of revealing to me and all who read this book that NOTHING is impossible of Him. With faith a mountain will move if I ask. The tiny tree was growing on a tree that had lost all its leaves. It was growing on the tree and pointed its tiny limbs in praise to heaven.

119

Nothing, you see, is impossible with God.
(Luke 1:37, The Message)

My journey took a little longer today, but it was worth it. Thank You, Lord Jesus Christ, my Father in the times of wonder. Thank You, Lord, for teaching me once again to let You be my guide, not me being Yours. Amen.

Chapter Twenty-Six

Family Visit

A woman's family is held together by her wisdom, but it can be destroyed by her foolishness.

(Proverbs 14:1, CEV)

Family gatherings are one of the most important and joyous parts of a holiday. The children, grandchildren, sisters, nieces and nephews all come together to give thanks and to celebrate the season. A holiday season God has so gracefully granted us to gather in His Name. The house is bursting with friends coming to see the ones they had not seen over the years. All of the doors are swinging back and forth in the busyness of human traffic. And the coolness of winter fills the room from the spinning doors. The season smells as the holiday favorites fill the nose of each person who comes through the rotating doors. The sounds and excitement of the children please, as well, as tire out the older ones. Praises and thanksgiving surround the small beautiful table with the young and old who have gathered.

Washing machine motions, dryer sounds, and pleasant smells from the clean and crisp clothes are many of the welcoming things holidays brings. Spills on the hardwood floors, water rings on freshly shined glass tables, water glasses in the sink, crumbs on the counter tops, and sticky spots you step into on the floor, these are nuisances, but they come with the joy of family gathering. "I want the red sleeping bag; I want the soft but firm bed; I want the couch in the den so I can watch TV, and please keep the noise down so we can sleep," are the sounds which come with family fun.

This Thanksgiving holiday was one of fun, tiredness and sore feet, short night sleeps, early morning calls, empty coffee pots, and many pans of biscuits. But, this comes with family love. Family love comes with many things that are worn on the feet but put love in the heart. "Grandmamma I am hungry! Can I help you cook? Will you make my animal biscuits, Grandmamma, so I can eat the eyes first?" are sweet sounds of grandchildren.

This holiday was busy and fast. The house was full and the sounds were that of a caring family. Since this was a holiday week, I found myself not looking or asking God what He wanted me to learn over the past three or four days. But I did not have to ask because my oldest grandson asked it for me. When we got up this morning he looked out the door and saw blackbirds invading the yard. He came to me before I started cooking and said, "Grandmamma, why do all those blackbirds come to this yard?" I said, "Well, maybe because they know they will find some food in this yard. And maybe they know we will not harm them."

After he asked me that question, I went to the back door and looked out. Sure enough blackbirds were overrunning the yard. They were walking about without fear. I opened the back door to see if they would move when they heard the door open, but they did not. They kept walking about eating whatever was in the grass. I went back to the kitchen to cook and forgot all about the birds, and we enjoyed each other.

The family members are gone and everything is quiet again. With the house so quieted I am lonesome for them and hope they come back soon for the Christmas holiday. Only this time, there will be many more family members in the house, and more for John and me to do. The washing machine will be cleaning many more loads of clothes. The doors will have many more dirty fingerprints on them from opening and closing so many times. The noise level will be shooting off the rickter scale. Our night's sleep will be cut to less than is needed by us. After everyone leaves, we will fall out and sleep for five or six days. When they come again many pans of biscuits will grace the breakfast table with all the trimmings to meet the many different needs. Is this hard work? Yes. Work is an example of our love for our family and friends. It is also an example of how God loves us. There is nothing too good for us, because He is our Heavenly Father. Is this something that is needed to be done? Yes, because it shows love by example. Jesus showed His love for us on Calvary.

CLEANING

When everyone leaves, the house always needs a good cleaning. In the afternoon after the house is clear of people I sit back and rest. At the beginning of the next day I get up to clean. I start in one of my least favorite rooms, the living room. I dust, and dust, and dust. I clean mirrors, mirrors, mirrors, and mirrors. I spray and clean pictures, pictures, and more pictures. I go from room to room doing the same thing in each over and over. I spray and shine the counter tops, islands, and stoves. I clean blinds and windows in the inside. I clean dust from the baseboards and the legs on the chairs. I clean figurines of old, and figurines just given, and more, more, more, more. I sweep and John mops the floors. All of the sticky stuff and spilled drinks and food are removed.

Next, but not last, I get to my daughter's old room. Now the real picking and pushing starts. There will be shoes under the bed. Our youngest grandson's pants will be under the bed and pillows on the bed seat. There will be rollers on the dresser and lotion out of place. The night light will be pushed to the side of the dresser and the children's toys with be here and there. This is the room where most of my exercise of the day takes place. If I did not have a chance to walk that morning, this room would make up for it. I get on my knees to see what is hidden under the bed, the dresser, the nightstand, and any other place anything can find a place to hide. The mirrors are cleaned of smudges from the children looking at themselves while brushing their teeth. The blinds are dusted of fingerprints that found their way there. The dresser is polished. The pictures are sprayed and cleaned. The dresser drawers are put back in place. The socks are replaced in the proper place. John always looks for his socks that our oldest grandson borrowed for church. Their clothes are washed and put in their drawers for their next visit. Then, I finish this overly-used room until the next time.

Over and over again I say, why in the world is this room looking like a war zone? I taught my daughter better than this. I have always kept a clean and orderly home. This room was clean before she got here, why is it looking like this now? Then I stop and listen to myself. Why this? Why that? Do I do the things the way God wants me to do them? Did God not give me the Word and examples of looking beyond the fault and seeing the need? Did God not give Himself as an example of His love for me, when I did not deserve it? Do I mess up, and He cleans it up for me? Have I put things aside when I should have picked them up and followed God? When I leave things out of place, and I know better, doesn't God give me a chance to get it right? When

I was lost in the ugly world of sin, did He not come into my room and clean me up?

Now, I have stopped complaining. I just go into the room and make sure it is clean and neat for her next visit home. When she comes, I am glad and thankful to have a loving and caring daughter- a daughter, who would give me her last dime if I needed it. She is a daughter who cares for her children and loves them as I love her,a daughter who will drive hours just to see our faces, and a daughter who is working to get closer to the Lord,the Heavenly Father, who supplies all of her needs. If the room is junky every time she comes, I will clean it and be glad to have her come again.

Why do we miss the things which cause us to work so hard and to lose sleep from the busyness of the crowds?

Once, I thought about what my grandchild had said about the blackbirds coming into the yard. I began to think about how we can go to our Heavenly Father when we are hungry and need food. But He wants the noise we make to be sounds of praises. Praises for giving us the chance to come to Him with our needs. Also, to be thankful that we can look to the One, who can fill our plates. We need to go without fear, but with reverence and thanks. God wants us to come as we have gone to our parents for help. And our children and grandchildren come to us knowing we will do all we can to meet their needs. We go with confidence and with assurance that we can find what we need from Him. We need to go to God with assurance that He loves us when all the others have turned their backs on us. When we gather together as His family of Christians, He takes pleasure in knowing we have gathered together as family. God wants us to be as a family. Just as we love for our children to come together as a family with love and thanksgiving.

When the family cleared out I missed them as soon as they were out of sight. My family was out of my sight but still on my heart. I am never out of God's sight; I am surrounded with His hedge of protection. He sees me when I am not walking and opening the right doors as He has directed me to do. But the blessing about God is that He forgives me when my room is messy!

Father, Lord Jesus Christ, please forgive me for my many short-comings. When I am in trouble, You are right there. When I am hungry, You fill my plate. When I mess up, You clean up the mess. Father, thank You for giving me chance and chance again to correct the mistakes I have made in this life. Amen.

Chapter Twenty-Seven

Sweet Sight

Thank You, Father, for this breathtaking cold and clear morning. Thank You for the bright and soothing sunshine. Thank You, Lord, for the white covering on the grass. Thank You, Lord, for the beautiful sight only You, Lord, can make and give. Lord, all my praises and thanks I give only to You. Lord Jesus Christ, hear and receive my humble prayer. Amen.

Lord, what a beautiful day you have waken me to this wonderful and cold morning. As soon as I looked out this morning I knew what the Lord wanted me to see in His glorious way. The housetops were covered in white with the morning frost. The grass was sparkling as if snow had fallen on it. The trees were sparkling in the midst of the white frost. The white fence was dull against the frost.

When John got up and looked out the window he let out a "Woo wee, look at that sight. Look how pretty it is out here this morning. It looks like snow out here!" I hurried to the window to look out, and it did look just like snow. Everything was covered with whiteness. The building, grass, trees, and even the pond were dancing in whiteness.

How beautiful it was just standing there looking at the morning beauty. My eyes could not conceive of all they were seeing. My heart danced with joy and excitement just looking at God's gift this blessed morning.

I went back to my bedroom to make the bed and to get myself ready for the day. After I finished I returned to the bathroom window to look out at the frost again, and it had begun to melt. I looked for a short time and returned to my bedroom to finish cleaning it. By the time I got back to the bathroom window most of the frost was gone. I looked out for a few minutes and returned to the bedroom to get my clothes so I could take my bath.

After I bathed and put my clothes on, I went to the kitchen to get breakfast ready for John and me. After breakfast, I went out to get the mail and all of the frost was gone. I looked at the grass and the trees and they were swaying in the morning breeze. The melted frost was dripping from each limb. The melted drops of frost were glinting in the sunlight as the morning sun dried it away.

As I walked to the mailbox, the sun was shining so brightly it broke the coldness of the morning. The sun was warm and relaxing on my face. I walked and looked at the empty, leafless trees. Most of the leaves were lying on the ground dried and withered from being detached from the trees. The few leaves still attached to the trees were blowing in the wind. Some of the smaller leaves were swaying with the motion of a butterfly. When I first noticed a small leaf moving in the breeze I thought it was a butterfly on the upper limb. The sides were moving so quickly that it resembled the movement of butterfly wings. It moved faster and faster, and then it moved even faster. I looked up at another leaf and it was moving with the same motion. I glanced at its size. It was small also. I noticed the larger leaves were not moving that fast. They moved in a slow and motionless sway. I stood and looked for awhile and the small leaves were still moving like butterflies, but they never fell from the tree.

After observing the small leaves for awhile, I noticed they were near the very top of the tree. Their little leaf wings were in motion with the breeze, and the very tip of the leaf was pointing upward. The leaves seemed as if they were spreading their little leaf wings straight up to heaven. They were moving as if giving thanks and praises to their Creator. "If man doesn't praise Me the trees and rocks will." I could sense the Lord saying these words to me.

How sad I felt when I looked at the leaves giving praises to the Lord and I failed to do so myself. When I am in church, I very seldom raise my hands in praise to God. I feel it in my heart, but God wants me to do more to praise His Name with action. He wants me to be an example of His blessings and how He is working in my life. God wants me to lift my voice in praise to Him also. I am so busy trying to please man with the voice God has given me, rather than giving all I can give to Him when I am singing His praises. For so many years I have worried about what the members of the church would think about my singing. Now, I care more about what God thinks of my singing. God knows my heart. He knows when I am giving Him all I have when I am praising Him. Making a joyful noise to the Lord is required of me.

Thank you little leaf for showing me what God wants me to do for Him. Thank You, Lord, for showing me what You want me to do to praise Your Holy and Mighty Name.

When I walked back into the house, I started to take out all of my Christmas decorations so I could put up my Christmas tree. The tree was pretty in color and shape. The lights were glinting white and its beautiful color sparks were dazzling. The dazzling lights were as lovely as the morning sun striking the frost. When the lights hit the tree decorations all of them sparkled brightly and clear in color. The lights were casting a beautiful glow similar to sunrays. The glass snowflakes were all covered in white frost. Oh, how pretty those frosty flakes looked on the tree. The clean and calming sight of the morning frost was calming and peaceful to look upon. To wake up to fresh fallen frost was one of God's wintry ways of wiping out some of the germs and giving nature a long awaited rest-a long awaited rest which the warm temperatures had held off. On a cold wintry night Jesus was born to wipe away our sins, so we could have a chance to rest in a heavenly home free of all illnesses and fears.

It was late afternoon when I finished getting the tree up. All the lights were blinking in a rhythmic movement. The lights were glowing through the glass figurines. The glow was that of a late afternoon winter sunset.

I sat a short while and looked at the comforting lights. Then I went outside to look at the sunset. The sky was a beautiful array of colors. The sun was casting a lovely pinkish purple flow. There were so many amazing colors my eyes could not conceive of all of them. The sky was decorated in the many colors made by God's hands.

After looking at the view of the sunset, I came back into the house. The lights on the tree were giving off some of the same colors of the sunset. Instantly, all of my praises went up to the Lord for His gifts of beauty. By sending His Son, Jesus Christ, on a cold winter night similar to this night, God's gift of His love for us came to earth. God calms our minds with His gifts of the beautiful things of nature. We cannot do anything apart from God. It is our gift of assurance that He is our protector. Most of all, I am thankful because He let me know He was guiding my steps as I was decorating for His Son, Jesus' birthday.

When I looked at the tree and all the other decorations, I could see everything God had revealed to me during the day. I could see the frost in the frosty lights and snowflakes. I could see the sunrays in the tree with lights sparkling through the branches. I could see the sunset in the glow of the lights on the houses next door. The lighted wreaths shone through the darkness like the evening star. You could see it shining from a distance welcoming family and friends to come and see its beauty.

The night was getting very chilly from the falling temperatures of this December night. I had my arms folded across my chest trying to keep warm, while looking at the lovely sight of the Christmas lights in the windows. I stood shaking from the cold for a few minutes, but the sights were so breath taking I stood awhile longer. The lights on each of the houses next door, and the shiny moon and stars were a friendly sight. But then my mind reflected on the many people who were homeless and cold. I thought about the ones who were without family and friends. I thought about the ones who are still in darkness and refused to see the beautiful light of God. I thought about the ones who give no thought to the beauty of God around us and about the ones who take the rain, sun, grass, and the singing of the birds for granted. I thought about the ones who are deaf to God's words. I thought about the ones whose minds are too closed to conceive the works of the Almighty God. I thought about the ones who do not feel the Lord's breath on their skin when the wind blows. I thought about the ones who will not let themselves hear the Lord's voice in the breeze.

Then, my body became too chilly. I rushed back into the house. The warmth and dryness of the house met me at the door. A weary and sad thought covered me. It covered me again. It covered me with the thoughts of the ones who were cold and wet. I sat in my chair and my mind went to Bethlehem and the night of Jesus' birth. Oh, how He loved me to give up a warm and beautiful home in heaven to come and be born in a place without heat. It was a place where the dampness crept in and chilled His body. Where there were no doors to close out the wind and snow, where there was no warm heat from the heater, and warm water to make His mother a warm glass of tea. I was weary and thankful because I know how much I am loved by the Almighty God. I am loved so much that He was born in a cold stable. How wonderful, marvelous, great, magnificent, superb, amazing, and merciful to have such love from the Father of Love. All the adjectives in the world cannot give enough thanks for the marvelous things God has done for me.

"Look at My sun and know I give light to My children. Look at the moon and stars and know I am with you when times seem dark. Look at the morning frost, and know that I will cleanse your sins if you come to Me. Look at the leaves fluffing in the breeze and know I give you the breath to breathe. I am the Breath of Life to the ones who love Me and keep My commandments. Look at My sunset and know I have blessings for you more than the colors of the sunrays. Look at the colors of the sunset and know there is a heavenly home waiting for you that is more beautiful than any sunset you can conceive. Be my light and let it shine brighter and more beautifully than the lights you have put on the tree. Be my branches to reach out to the ones who need to hear My words. Be My light to shine through the dark for others to follow. Hear My words and keep them as My gift to you. Be My Christmas gift for the world to see and hear My love for them. You are the spiritual tree to serve others. Be rooted and grow in My grace and understanding."

CHAPTER TWENTY-EIGHT

Ripping Waves

Father, Lord Jesus, here I am asking for Your forgiveness once again. Father, I need Your forgiveness for my constant complaining this holiday. There is no excuse that I can think of for my complaining. You and You alone want family together to be close and loving. Father, I love my family, but I have a poor way of showing my love and care this week. Father, forgive me for not letting my family see You in me. I am a poor example of Your love and mercy. Father, You want all of Your servants to be an example of Your love and of Your faithfulness. So, Father please forgive me for my shortcomings. Forgive me for not letting Your light shine through me. Forgive me for not turning to You once again. Father, it is so easy to say I am a shining light for You, until I am faced with temptations and doubt. Father, I know all I have to do is turn to You for my help. Father, if it is Your will, let me once again be a shining light for You. Father hear and receive my prayer in Your holy and precious Name I pray, Amen.

Consider it pure joy, my brother, wherever you face trials of many kinds.

(James 1:2)

What a week! What a week!

I love the Christmas season, so why do I work myself up so much? I run this way and that way. Something I promised myself I would not do this year. I did very well with my running and planning. The only thing I planned on doing was to have a good time in the Lord. Everything fell in place, or so I thought. The food was cooked and ready for my family. The house was clean and warm. The family members arrived safely. What more could I ask for this season? Did I say what else could I ask for this season?

Well, I will tell you...a clean house! People were here and there. Clothes filled the laundry room. Dishes were in the sink. Pans were left on the stove from making hot tea. Dry grass and mud spots were on the floor. Sweeping became a never-ending task. Blankets covered the chairs. Clothes covered the bed. Shoes were hidden under the chair. Where are my keys? Where did I put my glasses? Where did I put my purse? When will we eat? I am hungry. Can I have some chicken at 10:00 p.m.? I am cold. The water is cold. What is wrong with this television? Can we look at the cartoon channel? These are the sounds of family visits, but oh, how tired one becomes when things are out of the usual routine. And this was out of the routine for John and me.

So, rather than turning to the Lord for guidance, I decided to handle everything myself. Mistake, mistake, mistake! Being a person of organization, it soon became a problem for me. I like things where they belong. I like to have a clean kitchen. When John and I finish eating our dinner, the kitchen is cleaned and there is no more eating, and no more dishes are in the sink.

I walked around and picked up all the things laying on the chairs and beds. I put away dishes and closed cabinet doors. I picked up clothes from the bathroom. I put the blankets back where they belonged. My strength began to leave. My night's sleep was cut in half. My meditation was cut completely. My daily walk with God was cut. My daily devotion cut. Whose fault was it? Mine. Why? Because no one can keep you from the Lord, but you yourself. Because of my lack of commitment-my pure joy left.

After a morning of complaining I felt far away from God. I did not like that feeling, so I went outside to have a talk with God. God, what do You want me to see this day? And Father, I am sorry for the complaining I have been doing over the past few days. Lord, do not leave me. As I walked I heard sounds coming from the top of the trees I was walking under. I looked up and the sight of two woodpeckers calling to each others while flying from limb to limb filled my mind with joy. The sight was pleasant and comforting to see. Lord, what do you want me to learn?

One woodpecker flew to one tree and the other flew to another tree. As each went from limb to limb on its preferred tree, they were calling to each other as if to say "Come on over." I looked for awhile, and the sight of each bird was wonderful to behold. The red color on the top of each of their heads was beautiful. The feathers were white with black stripes. I looked and smiled. How wonderful and beautiful God's Creation is!

As I walked to get the paper, I was thinking about all of my complaining and whining. God had just shown me the beautiful sight of the woodpeckers and they were enjoying the limbs of the tree God had provided. Then I thought again, these birds never come this close to the house when I am out here. But this day they were flying around as if I were not there.

135

When I went back into the house I could still hear the sounds of the woodpeckers in my head. The sounds were calming. The calmness of the sound seemed, as if it was the voice of God telling me to be still because He was not pleased with the cranky way I had been acting. The sight of the woodpeckers seemed as if it was God showing me that there is a better way of dealing with a house full of guests. The woodpeckers were enjoying the presence of each other. They were communicating with joyfulness as they worked and played together.

My spirit was looking up with excitement and joy. I was so thankful the Lord had given me another chance to ask for forgiveness. As I sat at the table eating, my eyes caught the movement of a leaf whose stem was stuck in the crack of the floor of the porch. It was moving back and forward. As it moved the leaf was curved in the shape of wings. The wings were folding in and out. As they folded forward it seemed as if it was bowing in praise. When they folded backward, it seemed as if they were reaching toward heaven. The stem was stuck tightly and firm in the crack. When the wind blew it, it moved with the wind. It moved left, right, backward, and forward. As I looked, I asked the Lord once more what He wanted me to see from the leaf.

Then all at once I knew the Lord was showing me that I cannot stray from His path because I am facing a different situation in my house. I must be able to move with the waves of life. But when he asks, he must believe and not doubt, because he who doubst is like a wave of the sea, blown and tossed by the wind (James 1:6). The leaf was rooted in the crack and the wind could not move it from where it was stuck. Immovable is what God wants me to be in my faith. When change comes and it moves me right, left, backward or forward I must be able to stand.

Not only did God reveal the woodpeckers and leaf, He carried my mind back to the view I saw when I got up this morning. When I opened the northern curtains, my eyes landed on a sight of ducks floating on the pool. They were floating in formation on the pool. Two were floating together and ten others were floating and ducking in the water. As I watched the ducks, some would disappear under the water, but the waves would reveal where each was. The waves would move completely across the pool. Then as the waves would calm down, the ducks would come up. I watched for awhile longer and the ducks did the same thing over and over again. Each time one went under the water the waves covered the pool.

I moved from the window to open the other windows in the house. When I returned to the window, the ducks were gone for the day. As the day moved on, God revealed to me that I cannot duck and hide from my problems, but need to turn to Him. When I try to handle them myself all I am doing is making a lot of rippers and waves, which solves nothing. When the waves calm down, the problems resurface and nothing is solved. Also when I let the Lord handle my worries, He will let them all roll off me like the water on a duck's back.

The woodpeckers are my reminder that family is wonderful even with my house out of order. The leaf is for me to stand on God's words, and I cannot duck and hide from my problems.

My house is clean and in order because my sister helped me to get it back the way I like it. But in the process, I had to go through all of the complaining and missing an opportunity to enjoy my family the way I should have. I am watching my grandchildren, nieces and nephews play as I type. The sound of children certainly is God's plan of PURE JOY. I am thankful God and my sister helped me to realize what I was missing this Christmas Season.

•

Chapter Twenty-Nine

In God's Arms

Dear Heavenly Father, thank You for giving me my dreams back. Thank You for forgiving me once again. Father, forgive me for my shortcomings and whining. Father, guide me through this day, and please keep a hedge around my children and family. Father, thank You for the happiness You have put back into my heart. Father, hear and receive my prayer, in Your Holy Name, Amen.

What a beautiful day the Lord has given us! The weather is cold but refreshing. The ducks are floating on the pool in a graceful formation and beauty. The sky is cloudy, but glorious to look upon. The birds are flying and singing overhead. Oh, how wonderful it is to see God's creation and wonders working according to His will! Father, I am thankful once again to be one of Your humble servants.

As I walked around the yard this morning, everything was calm and beautiful. The water in the pool was calm with soft rippling movements. Two ducks were flowing on the rippers. Then all at once a whooping crane flew up from the corner of the pool. My eyes were watching in amazement because it came up quickly and gracefully without warning. Its wings were wide and lovely. The motion of the wings was slow in movement, and pleasant to look upon.

Everytime I get in a close view of the crane it flies away. It flees from danger to a place it thinks is safe whenever I come near it. Looking at its quick flight, I began to think how we can flee to a place of safety in the Lord. The crane was flying away from danger just as we should flee away from the danger of sin.

I thought more and more about how the Lord is a place of protection when the deceiver tries to snare us. When we sense danger, we should not wait to see what will happen; we should flee from it before it gets too close.

Also, not only did the crane remind me of fleeing to safely, it reminded me of how quickly sin can overtake us. The crane flew up from the water without warning. I did not see it before it flew up, but it saw me.

With all my heart I praise the Lord, and with all that I am I praise his holy Name! With all my heart I praise the Lord! I will never forget how kind he has been.
(Psalm 103:1-2)

CHAPTER THIRTY

Arm in Arm

Lord, listen to Your children praying. Lord, bring Your Spirit in this place. Lord, listen to Your children praying. Send them love, send them power, and send them grace.

By Ken Medema

Father, thank You for this warm and cloudy day. Thank You for giving me another chance to see Your wonderful works in action. Father, thank You for waking me this blessed morning. Thank You, Lord, for Your saving power and mercy. Father, keep my family and friends through this day as we travel to and from doing Your Holy will. These are the blessings I am asking in Your precious Name, Amen.

What a beautiful day this first Tuesday in this new year of 2005 is! The day is lovely with the clouds barely covering the sun. The warm breeze met my face with a pleasant caress. The feel of the soft gentle wind carried me into a state of worship right away. As the wind caressed my skin the Holy Spirit directed my eyes to the sky. My hands went up in praise and thanks to the Almighty for His tender loving care. My hands were swaying higher and higher in the wind like a kite on a windy March day. "Oh, thank

You, Lord, for Your love! Thank You, Lord, for giving me sight and hearing to see Your face amidst Your creations, and to hear the serene singing of the wind in the trees. I praise You, Lord, this morning; I give You all of my praises. Praise You, Lord, for Your goodness. I praise You, Lord, for bringing me to this point in my life to give You praises without fear of being heard by others. Thank You for giving me a chance to say thank You once again for Your kindness.

Lord, what do You want me to see this morning? Father, will today be the ending of this book? Father, just let me thank You once again for loving me! Lord Jesus Christ, I love You because You are worthy of all my love. I want to thank You for loving me first, Father. Thank You, Father for all of Your blessings and forgiveness.

My hands and arms were flapping in the air like a fat kite without a string. I was filled with thanksgiving and gratefulness. I walked away from the backyard after giving thanks, and went to the paper box to get the paper. As I was walking, I heard the flutter and sounds of mourning doves. They were flying from tree to tree, then they flew out of my sight. I walked on to the box. Then I heard the sound of more birds. Some were bluejays; one was a robin; some were bluebirds.

I stood and watched the birds playing together under the same tree. Some were playing amongst themselves and others were walking around under the tree. The bluebirds walked around pecking the ground for food. The robin walked over to eat where the bluejays were playing. Then all at once, one of the bluejays swooped down on the robin. The robin flew up in a large tree away from the attacking bluejay. The robin sat on one of the limbs and within seconds another bluejay swooped at it. The robin flew to another tree, then another bluejay swooped at it. The robin flew as fast as it could into the woods with another bluejay in pursuit. The robin stayed in the woods for awhile, and then when I turned around, it flew back into the yard with another bluejay trailing it.

When the robin got back in the yard, another bluejay flew after it. Awhile later all of the bluejays swooped onto the robin. They kept after the robin until it was completely out of the yard. All of the bluejays followed it until it was out of the area where the blue-jays were playing, and completely out of their sight.

After the robin was gone, all of the bluejays came back to the yard and began to play with each other. They played together like children playing tag. One would jump in front of the other, and then the other one would block its path. What a peaceful sight to be a part of and to behold the courageous protection the birds were giving one another.

I stood and watched for awhile to see what would happen if the robin came back into the yard, but it never returned while I was standing there. As I was walking to the house, the Lord revealed to me that we as His children should fight together in His Name. We should stand and fight together against sin. When we see sin in our midst, we should fight together to chase it away from us. We should bind together arm in arm to not let sin and wrongs stay among us. He wants us to work together so when one of us grows weak the other is there to give strength. We need to pray together so the evil one cannot stay among us in peace. If we will fight together like the bluejays, this world will be a better place for all of God's children. We need to chase worries and wrongs away until you cannot see them any longer. The bluejays formed a bluejay net of protection for each other. We need to form an arm to arm chain of protection for each other to remain strong and faithful.

The bluejays were a simple example of working together in one accord. The robin did not have a chance to settle among the blue-jays because they did not allow it to get comfortable. How many mountains would move if we worked and prayed in one accord? When we see things which are not pleasing to God, we need to swoop down on it together until it is gone from our sight and not let its wrongs rest and get comfortable among us. Then we will be able to once again walk our streets without worries. We will be able to let our children play as children should play without worries of being harmed. Illness will flee, joy will increase, and love for our fellowman will be widespread because the evil one will not be able to stay in the midst of us and survive.

> *The Name of the Lord is a strong tower; the righteous run to it and are safe.*
>
> (Proverbs 18:10)

> *You will laugh at destruction and famine, and need not fear the beasts of the earth.*
>
> (Job 5:22)

> *The Lord will keep you from all harm-he will watch over your life.*
>
> (Psalm 121:7)

> *Who is going to harm you if you are eager to do good?*
> (I Peter 3:13)

How wonderful it is to be able to see God at work in the midst of His little creatures, and to learn a much-needed lesson:

> *The Lord All-Powerful is with us. The God of Jacob is our fortress.*
>
> (Psalm 46:11)

> *You are my hiding place; you will protect me from trouble and surround me with songs of deliverance.*
>
> (Psalm 32:7)

144

CHAPTER THIRTY-ONE

Two by Two

*Later, Jesus appeared in another form to two disciples,
as they were on their way out of the city.*

(Mark 16:12)

*Then he called together his twelve apostles and sent
them out two by two.*

(Mark 6:7)

Father, thank You for this blessed day. This is a day that I have never seen before, and will never see again. Father, let me live the best I can live for You this day. Let me be a blessing to others in Your Name, Amen.

Have you stopped and really seen the trees, birds, water, grass, flowers, and the movement of the wind, the changing of the seasons, and the ducks and wild geese floating on the water? These are only a few of God's wonders.

This morning as I was taking my morning walk, I noticed the wild ducks floating on the pond. They were gliding in a graceful movement. They were in pairs of twos or groups of threes. Each pair moved in its own direction. One pair would move north and the other group to the south. Then each would turn and glide east and west. When one would stop to take a dive, the other one would wait until it came up. Sometimes two would dive together when the other pair would come in their direction. I noticed the pair would not dive together if the other pair was not near.

I stood and watched for awhile as the ducks floated alone on the pond. The ripples in the water were in a graceful pattern. As the ducks were moving from one side to the other, I put my arms on the fence and laid my head in them as I watched. I stood there and stared and stared. My heart was rejoicing as I observed them. The amazement of God's creation was blessing me as I looked. My tiredness from the holiday seemed to dive also into the water as the ducks were diving. I was being washed in the glory of the Lord the longer I lingered there.

Later as I stood there, one of the ducks in the group of three, drifted behind. It floated on the water all by itself. It moved a little one way and then a little another way. Then I noticed something else. The pair of twos stayed near by it. The other two ducks that were in the pair with the drifting one, only went a short way from it. Each group had it hedged in from each side. Neither of the groups moved too far from the one duck. After the duck floated by itself for awhile, the group that it was with came back to it, and also the other pair. Each group stayed close to the one duck, and then all the ducks floated in a picturesque formation together.

As I looked, I started to think about how Jesus sent His apostles out two by two to do His will. Then I looked at my neighbor's house and the others houses near mine. I looked at the ducks again and at my neighbor's houses again. Then I began to think how all of the other ducks were surrounding the one duck. They did not leave it until it decided to come back into the group.

How often do I visit my neighbors when they are in need? How often do I look after their home when they are not there? How often do I pray for them when they are sick? How often do I know if they are sick? It troubled my heart to know that I am not a better neighbor. I looked at the ducks again and they were still floating in a beautiful formation on the pond. They were working together. They were protecting each other. One was diving while the other watched. Do I watch out for my neighbors?

I began to think how the Lord never leaves me when I stray from Him. He puts His angels about me to shield me from harm. When I stray from His path, He picks me up and forgives me again. When I am sinking in the sea of sin, He is there when I decide I want to come back. When I think I am floating along on the pond of troubles, He is there watching over me to make sure I do not get lost. When I am in danger, He has me covered in the front, the back, and the sides; He is my rear guard (Isaiah 52:12). God went into hell to save me. I am washed clean with His blood. What a glorious day! It is glorious because I never have to float through this life alone. I have my Father, Jesus Christ, in my group.

The Lord forgives our sins, heals us when we are sick, and protects us from death. His kindness and love are a crown on our heads. Each day that we live, he provides for our needs and gives us the strength of a young eagle. For all who are mistreated, the Lord brings justice.
(Psalm 103:1-6, CEV)

147

CHAPTER THIRTY-TWO

I Hear You, Lord

Everyone with good sense wants to learn. It's stupid and embarrassing to give an answer before you listen. Being cheerful helps when we are sick, but nothing helps when we give up.

(Proverb 18:13-15, CEV)

As I was walking about this morning seeking to hear the words of the Lord, a beautiful sound from the morning finches met my ears. I have been hearing the singing of the finches since the blooms began to come on the many trees around the yard. But to my deaf ear and blinding eyes, I would not let my senses hear the voice of the Lord for today's lesson.

What do you want me to see this morning, Lord? As I walked among the tall overgrown beautiful green grass in the yard, I kept asking the Lord for an answer. The grass was tall because the rain had fed the grass with the food it needed to grow wonderfully tall. As I walked I was in search of the thing or things God wanted me to see. You are all-seeing and all-knowing, Father. Help me to see You today.

I walked and began to pray aloud in the spirit. Lord, what do You want me to put on these last pages of this book? Lord, what do You want me to see this sunny spring day? What Lord? What? Then within seconds the beautiful sounds of the finches singing in the trees filled the portals of my mind. What a glorious sound. The melody filled the depths of my ears, and the breathtaking sounds lifted my praises higher and higher to the Lord. The sounds filled the portals of my mind which had been searching for the sounds and sights of the Lord's wonderful Creation.

As I looked up to the trees, the leaves were swaying magnificently with the cool breeze of spring. The leaves were yellow and green in color-the colors only God's hands can make. With the movement of the leaves and the sound of finches, one would have thought the leaves were singing a heavenly song. Oh, the sounds were glorious! My praises to God lifted even higher. Higher and higher I lifted my hands in thanksgiving to the One and only Maker of such music, my Lord and Savior Jesus Christ. Thank You, Lord, for this sight and sound. Only You, Lord, can give such peace and contentment to a searching mind.

Lord, I know now what you want me to write. I know, because I hear Your messengers.

The winds are your messengers, and flames of fire are your servants.
(Psalm 104:4,CEV)

As I looked up into the trees, I could hear the sounds and songs of the finches, but I could not see them. The finches and the leaves on the trees were the same color. The leaves were the finches' shields from the enemy. The leaves were their protection from harm because God made them in such a way that the eyes of the enemy could not see anything but the movement of leaves.

The finches and leaves blended together so the color would be the same. The leaves were their hiding place. Only the wonderful sounds of glorious music could be heard.

"I have you covered the same way the leaves are covering the birds with My holy Blood," the Lord said to me. "I am with you in times of trouble and joy. You cannot see Me, but I am right beside you. When the enemy comes against you, do not fear because you are covered with My protection."

I know Lord, I know. I walked and looked up again at the trees and all I could see were the movements of the beautiful colored leaves. All I could hear was the beautiful sounds of the finches singing. The sounds were like that of a heavenly choir. Joy filled my heart and forgiveness welled up in my heart. Lord, forgive me once again for not turning to You when things come against me. Forgive me for almost whining again. I promised You when you restored my breath I would always turn to You in my times of hurt. Lord, thank You for showing me once again how much You love and want to protect me even when I am not looking, and when I cannot see You. You always make Your presence known and I know I am covered.

From his holy temple, the Lord looked down at the earth.
He listened to the groans of prisoners, and he rescued
everyone who was doomed to die.
(Psalm 102:19-20, CEV)

Like the hawk, You revealed to me this morning, Lord, soaring high over the trees that You are all watchful. When trouble comes within my midst, You, Lord, are looking down on me from high above. Like the finches in the grass, I only know they are there when I walk among them and they soar to the sky. Even when my enemies are hidden from me, You are my tree of protection. You are my wings I take flight on. You are the leaves of the tree where I take refuge. I am invisible to my enemy like the finches in the trees. You are the hawk which soars high above spotting out and revealing my enemies. They flee from Your presence.

MY PROMISE

A year ago, my blood pressure was so out of control that I was on two to three blood pressure pills a day. To make sure it would not go up at night, I had to take one before I went to sleep that is, when I could sleep. I was taking a pill to help me sleep. And most of the time the pill for sleep did not work. To help the pill for sleep, a pill was added to calm the nerves in my aching hands and shoulders. My body consisted of medication and pain. Even with me taking pills to help out, another pill did not help. I constantly whined and complained, "Why me? I do not understand why I am going through these things." I could not sleep at night, and I could not sleep during the day! My enemy was getting the best of me. "Why me, Lord?" I whined. Why?

One frightening but blessed night, God worked a miracle in my life. He took my breath away. I could not breathe. I was jerking in my sleep when my husband woke me up. I awoke fighting for air and feeling as if I was floating on my face. I was fighting and fighting to breathe. I was floating on my face, so it felt, just trying to breathe. I was fighting, fighting to get back something precious- my precious breath. And then God restored the thing I could not live without, my breath. My wonderful breath. How good it felt to breathe again.

But then fear ran over me. I could not go back to sleep because I was so afraid. Now I understand the term "Shaking like a leaf on a Tree" I was shaking and also thankful to have my life

152

back (we cannot live without air and the ability to breathe it into our lungs). It was a miracle because John woke me up in his sleep. He was sleeping, but woke me up at the same time. Days went by and I was still afraid to go back to sleep. I was afraid I would stop breathing again. My blood pressure medication had caused the reaction.

After a few nights of being afraid to sleep, I finally did with the help of another pill. Some months passed, and I was still taking medication to sleep. Then the Lord came to me in a dream.

I went to bed with my sleep medication, but the Lord was ready for me to turn to Him, and Him alone. As I was sleeping, the Lord began to show me many animals in the clouds. They were moving about as if in a slide picture show. In each slide the Lord showed me a different animal. Then my husband began to fight with this a certain creature. I knew it was evil because it had a hook or claw hand. As my husband was fighting, he broke the claw off and told me and the children to run. Now, our children are grown, but they were still small children in the dream. As he fought, he yelled, "Run!" and we began to run. But I had the claw/hook in my hand which was broken off. As I ran, I knew the creature was going to hit me because I was clutching part of its hand. The creature grew back the part which was broken off and hit me in the back with it. I fell to the ground. My husband and children made it safely across the danger zone. As I laid there on my back, my eyes looked up to the sky and Jesus was looking down on me crying. Jesus was weeping over me. Jesus was as big as the space, but His weeping outpowered everything else.

When I woke the next morning I could not get the sight or feeling of what had gone on out of my mind. I went to Sunday school and told the class about my dream. Some shrugged it off as being nothing more than a mere dream. I told my pastor about my dream, and he shrugged it off. I called a pastor friend, and told her about my dream, but she did not understand it. I talked to my husband about it again, but I was never pleased with the answers I was getting. I needed to know what was going on. I kept asking and telling people about what I had dreamt. Some shrugged it off as being nothing; others wanted me to use a dream book For interpretation. I did not want to use the dream book. I needed the answer from the Lord. When I asked the Lord for my answer He gave it.

"What took you so long to turn to Me?" the Lord asked.

I was handling it myself.

DREAM REVEALED

God could not heal me because I was standing in the way. The night He took my breathe away He gave it back to me with His healing power in it. He breathed life back into my body, and my blood pressure was healed that night. The claw in my hands signified the worries I was carrying around. The whining and complaining was destroying my life here on earth and the chance to be with Him. Rather than giving God all of my worries and pains, I looked to man for the answers. God could not help me when I was holding on to hurt, pain, and despair. He could only lift me up from my circumstances when I would move out of the way. My soul was in jeopardy. God loved me too much to give up on me.

I had to forgive and to ask for forgiveness. I was holding onto the time people had misused me, and was not forgiving them. I had done something in my life that I had to ask forgiveness for. When I threw the hooks and claws away, God stepped in and my fears were released.

154

Since those nights, God has shown me many more dreams and visions. Some I still do not understand, but in time He will show me. He has put a word in my mouth that will not be silenced. The God and Father of my life is weeping for all of His lost souls. He is weeping because we will not allow Him to help us. He is weeping because we will not cry out to Him and ask for His help. He is weeping because He can carry all of our burdens, but we will not let Him.

With God restoring the very breath my enemy tried to cut short, I am one of the voices that will keep crying out His Name and continue to carry His word wherever I go.

For the one who is sick and needs to be healed, do not let whining keep you from the healing power of God. My voice will be used to tell the good news that God is waiting to be asked for His blessings.

God knew me before I was formed in my mother's womb. He knew what I was going to do; I had to take the long rough road when the easier one was so easy to travel. My whining kept me from the blessings of the Lord.

Thank You, Lord, for giving me the singing of the finches to remind me once again that You are my shelter even when I cannot see you. Thank You for loving me so much that You gave me back the breath and joy You had in store for me before I was formed. Father, our daily walks have given me the joy only You can give.

After a few days of listening and enjoying the sound of the finches, I could no longer hear them sing, even thought, I could see them as they played among the grass. Then the Lord said to me, "You cannot hear Me if your mind is cluttered with things I have not put there. Keep your mind fixed on Me." Certainly, I began to hear the lawn mower and not the finches. My neighbor's mower was drowning out the singing of the birds.

How often we miss the voice of the Lord because our minds are fixed on the sounds of the world. When I walked closer to the tree where the finches were singing, my mind only concentrated on the beauty of God's Creation. What a delightful moment with my Heavenly Father. The only One, Who, knows my needs. What a WONDERFUL GOD WE SERVE.

> *Nothing about me is hidden from you! I was secretly woven together deep in the earth below, but with your own eyes you saw my body being formed. Even before I was born, you had written in your book everything I would do.*
>
> (Psalm 139:15-16, CEV)

Chapter Thirty-Three

What Did it See in Me?

You made him ruler over the works of your hands; you put everything under his feet: all flocks and herds, and the beasts of the field, the birds of the air, and the fish of the sea, all that swim the paths of the seas.

(Psalm 8:6-8)

I thought as I was writing the ending of this book that the Lord has shown me the many things I needed to see and know to grow stronger in Him. But was I mistaken! A year has passed and I thought I was finished with this book, and it was ready to be printed. But God said, "You are not finished yet. There is something else you need to learn about walking in faith and trust." During the year I have read more of God's words and prayed for more understanding. God has shown me He wants me to only follow and seek after Him. This revelation took place through a little dog sent to our house.

Now you have to know me to understand why a little dog would make a different. I will not hurt any animal, but I do not want one touching me or me touching it. And for one to come into my house is a no-no because I am the "Queen of Clean!"

Now this took place around the middle of June when the weather was just cool enough to have the windows up in the house. Early, that morning I was standing in the window watching the morning sky and listening to the sounds of nature. As I was standing in front of the bathroom window enjoying the feel of the cool morning breeze on my face, a little dog came and sat under my window. I just stood there watching this little lady sit there. I did not say a word or make a sound, but all at once she looked up and saw me in the window looking down at her. She looked up at me a second time and began to cry out in fear. She ran from the window screaming with a high-pitched child like cry. I said, "Lord, what did she see in me to make her so frightened?" I felt bad because I want the love of God to show in me even to the animals.

I left the bathroom and went to open the blinds in my back bedroom. As I opened the blinds I heard the little dog walking on the porch under the bedroom window. I said, "Get off the porch. Get off the porch, now dog!" The little lady would not move. I went into the kitchen and got some vinegar water and sprayed it on the dog, she still would not move. I got the broom and pushed her. She still would not move. Then I just stood there and looked at the poor little thing. I turned to walk back in the house, and she followed right behind me. I turned again to say, "Get away from me!" but she still followed after me. To my surprise, I got some food from the table to give to the little lady. Why did I do that? Because she kept following me wherever I went. Later on in the morning, I sat in the rocking chair on the porch and it sat next to my feet. To tell the truth, the little fellow was so sweet looking and its coat was so shiny and pretty I could not help but like it.

My grandson came to the porch after he had gotten up and said, "Grandmamma, where did this dog come from? She does not have any fleas and she, has a pretty coat. You and granddad should keep her." I looked at him and said, "Ask your granddad." I knew John would say no. But was I surprised! John said, "Yes, we can keep her, because God sent this dog here." I was surprised again because he let the dog come into the house. I was surprised for the fourth and fifth time because I let the dog come into the house.

We gave that little dog three baths in one day, because if she was coming into my house she was going to be clean. Not only did we give her all those baths, we let her ride in the car. That night we let her sleep in the house. She slept right next to my bed. When I would get up to go to the bathroom she would follow me. She would sit at the door until I came out, then follow me back to the bed. When I would lie down she would lay next to my bed again.

Around daybreak, I heard her get up, but I continued to sleep. Around 6:00a.m. I got up to use the bath but she did not follow me this time and I knew why. When I opened the bathroom door a smell hit me that my senses had never smelled before. I looked to the left of me, and I knew why I never wanted a dog in my house. DOG POOP! I got the pet cleaner and started to clean the dog waste from my floor. But to my surprise again, I did not get upset. It was my fault that I did not let her out when I heard her walking in my house. She stayed in the house during the day, but that night she had to stay outside. During the night, we heard something jump up and hit the window. John looked out to find the dog jumping up to the back bedroom window where it first heard my voice. We heard her jumping and hitting the window until we fell a sleep. The next morning when we got up, dogprints were on the outside wall. The next night the same thing happened. On the third night we let her stay in the house again, but you can bet I got up and let her out when he started to walk.

The next week, we carried her to the vet for a check-up. This time, I was surprised more than the other times. The check-up for the dog cost more than my yearly checkup. We wrote the check and went to the pet store and to get her a bed. I could not believe that I would buy a dog bed, but I wanted her to be comfortable and to feel loved.

I was thinking what is wrong with me?

A few weeks later, I was rocking in the rocking chair and the Lord spoke to me about this little dog which my grandson had now named Frisky. He named her Frisky because she would run around and jump on people. She would roll around on the grass and then jump into the air. When Frisky first came she was frightened of me, but she took me as her master. A few days before she came to the house, a snake was lying on the walkway in front of the porch. The snake escaped and we did not know where it went. My grandson was afraid to walk on the walk, but my husband and I told him he had nothing to be afraid of, yet I still felt a little anxious. That afternoon after the dog came, John asked me to look up some information about dachshunds to see if they protected homes from pests:

"Dachshund is a pet, not a hunter, but still maintains the characteristics of independence, courage, hardiness, and combativeness that served so well as it challenged the fierce badger in its den. The other half of the Dachsie personality moderates its bold attitude with a loving demeanor, a heavy dose of charm, and a playful sense of humor."

After she arrived we did not see any more snakes or pests around the house.

We were sure more than ever that God put Frisky in our home. She was so sweet, yet protective of us. One day a man rode by on his bike and had been drinking. He had a beer bottle in his hand. When Frisky saw this man she began to bark and took on a defensive mode of attack. She stood at the end of the driveway so he could not come into the yard; we had to make her come away from the driveway. As I looked at her protecting the yard, I realized God was showing me how He was with me in the midst of storms.

When I correct Frisky, she still never leaves my side, she just humbles down and sits at my feet. With a humble spirit is the only way we can serve, and humbly ask forgiveness when we stumble in this life journey. When we leave the house she greets us when we drive into the yard. When we are in the presence of the Lord, we must greet Him with thanksgiving and praises.

I thought about how Frisky sleeps at my side at night and follows me to the bathroom during the night. I notice she never follows John when he moves, just me. Then I remembered reading that a "Dachshund sits at the master's feet and is protective of its master." We can only serve one Master if we want to sit at His feet in heaven. At Jesus' feet lies our strength to go through this life of trails and temptations. When I look at Frisky, she loves me even when I forget to feed her., I know even in my hurts, I love Jesus enough to go through the trials. He sends my way in order to carry out His Word. Frisky never leaves my side when I am in her presence. In Jesus' presence is protection and assurance that He is always at our side. All Frisky wants from me is a gentle touch and a rub on the head. All Jesus wants from us is our obedience. God put all this in motion to show us how He never leaves us. He is near us when we sleep. He is waiting at the door when we get up at night. He protects us from the enemy when he tries to come into the yard. He cleans up after us when we mess up, and forgives us for messing up. He still stays near when we do not feed ourselves with His Word. He is a gentle touch when we are hurting. He stays near and rocks us in His arms when we are afraid. When danger is around He guards the path where the enemy tries to come in. He guards the windows of our hearts so the world cannot come in. He knows our voice when we call. He fights the unseen snake that tries to creep in. He is kind yet, He is the Almighty.

Now, I know why Frisky cried out when she saw me. I was crying inside and the pain of all the doubts were showing on the outside. A little dog was sent to show me how my Father prepared a way for me when hurt was at my door. My friends call Frisky my godly dog, and I am thankful the Lord saw fit to put her under my bathroom window. Frisky exhibits all the characteristics a Christian should have – happy, humble, hears and obey the master's voice is protective of the Master (His Word), stays near the Master, sits at the Master's feet, serves only one Master, protects the yard (body, mind, and spirit) from the enemy, and fears and doubts are not a part of Jesus' plan for His children.

By reading this book you all know by now the bathroom is my favorite place to read and talk with the Lord early in the morning, and look what I found there – Frisky, my godly dog. Now I know what Frisky saw in me – a vessel still being molded by the Master's hands.

BIOGRAPHY

At a young age Herticine was passionate about her fellow classmates who were pushed aside because of their learning disability. This passion for the hunting led her to become a Special Education teacher. She taught with a strong desire to see her students' succeed in the classroom as well as life. Herticine taught for twenty one years until her health fail. However, her yearning for teaching left emptiness in her life until God led her to teach Bible study classes in her church and home. Her hunger for the Word of God increased in 2004-while struggling to fall asleep one night…while in immense pain Jesus appeared to her in a dream, He was looking down on her weeping; she knew something was wrong in her life if Jesus was weeping over her, and how much He must have loved her. After the dream she studied the Scriptures and searched for answers from God through His Word, fasting, and praying.

Shortly after God led her to look more closely at things He directed her to in hers surrounding. He was teaching her to seek Him through the simple things we so often take for granted. During a thirty –three day walk with God, He showed her how to see and hear the Creator through His creations. In 2006, God called Herticine by name to carry His Word to the ones seeking a deeper walk with Him, and she did.

Herticine echoes the word of Paul's:

I am not ashamed of the gospel, because it is the power of God for the salvation of everyone who believes.
(Romans 1:17)

Herticine and her husband, John live in Nettleton, Mississippi where they walk with God daily and view the gifts He reveals to them through nature. They have two children.

e United States
01B/124-315/A